After the Storm Comes the Rainbow

After the Storm Comes the Rainbow

PAUL H. DUNN

Bookcraft
Salt Lake City, Utah

Library of Congress Catalog Card Number: 88-72059

ISBN 0-88494-662-2

4th Printing, 1990

Printed in the United States of America

Contents

Preface

In a recent publication entitled *Variable Clouds, Occasional Rain, with a Promise of Sunshine,* I reminded the reader that life, like the weather, has its "gloomy days" filled with many challenges and setbacks. While we all experience a variety of personal storms, time and nature have a way of putting everything into proper perspective. It was Jonathan Edwards who said, "Surely there is something in the unruffled calm of nature that overawes our little anxieties and doubts: the sight of the deep-blue sky, and the clustering stars above, seem to impart a quiet to the mind." Goethe reminds us that "nature is the living visible garment of God."

Like nature, our lives can weather any and all frustrations we may experience and we will find, as Colton says, "the rainbow, that smiling daughter of the storm."

Lord Byron gives additional assurance when he counsels:

Be thou the rainbow to the storms of life,
The evening beam that smiles the clouds away,
And tints tomorrow with prophetic ray!

So it is that the principles of the gospel, when applied, are to the storms of life what the rainbow is to nature.

This volume is not a Church publication, and the author alone is responsible for its views and contents.

Again, I am deeply indebted to my wife, Jeanne, whose insights, suggestions, experiences, and genius with words has added a great dimension to this work. I am grateful to my daughter, Janet Gough, who took time to read the manuscript and made many appropriate comments. I am always grateful to my family for their constant encouragement.

I express my grateful appreciation once more to my able secretaries, Sharene Hansen and Elaine Seamen, for their wonderful assistance in the many details surrounding such a project. And to a special friend, David Christensen, I once again extend my thanks.

I also express great appreciation to Bookcraft for our long association and for their cooperation and professional manner in bringing this publication to a successful completion.

I

When the Storm Comes

Weathering the Storm

In the classic movie *The Sound of Music*, Julie Andrews—who plays the part of Maria, Captain Von Trapp's nanny for his seven children—wins their favor and trust by her great enthusiasm for life and concern for people. One great scene portrays Maria in the Von Trapp home one stormy night as she prepares to retire. The lightning and thunder are awesome and cause great concern and fright among the children. As all seven gather in her room for comfort and reassurance, she sings to them, "These are a few of my favorite things," and then proceeds to list them in song. As the children join in, fear gives way to calm and peace.

That great scene recalls an experience I once read about. Years ago, a columnist for a Wisconsin newspaper wrote this tribute to his mother the day she died: "She taught me to love the storm." He described how as a child he had been terrified of thunder and lightning. When the big, dark clouds came rolling in and the sound of thunder cracked outside his window, he used to hide in his closet, trembling. But his mother always came for him during these storms and, taking him by the hands, led him to the front porch where the heavenly violence could be seen in all its force. There she described the grandeur of a nature that could produce such things as the beauty of the jagged flashes of light across the sky. Gradually the boy "learned to love the storms, and all the things that make storms in life—controversy, reverses, criticism—no longer terrified him." My own mother, who had been so taught by her father, did a similar thing with us.

Storms are an inevitable part of weather. We simply couldn't exist on earth without the wind or the gray, damp days that bring us rain.

And storms are inevitable in each of our lives. Adversity is to life what stormy weather is to nature. Most of us have experienced some disappointment or heartache. A loved one dies, we face ill health, we miss an opportunity, we have a nagging worry, we are alone and we think nobody cares about us—all these things can make us feel as if the thunderclouds are gathering around us with crushing force.

How do we learn to live with our stormy days?

Frankly, some never do learn. Some people let reverses embitter them. They decide the world is a terrible place to be in and die long before they're buried.

A widow who had faced some setbacks in life just pulled her shades against the world. She became the neighborhood grouch, even going so far as to fill up with water cars that were accidentally parked in front of her house.

As one wit said, "You never know what makes some people tick until they begin to unwind."

But others handle their disappointments in life with far better grace. Take for instance the man who had been seriously ill with scarlet fever as a child and who was almost completely deaf from the beginning of his adolescence. At age six he accidentally set fire to his father's barn, for which he was whipped in public as an example to the other children.

His family was so poor that he couldn't go to school and was required to work at an early age. He was discharged from many of his jobs because he didn't fit in. And there were times when he existed for days on end with only one meal for lack of money.

Who was this man who apparently faced more than his share of life's stormy days? Thomas Edison —the same man who said that he had discovered a thousand things that didn't work before he found the right material for the filament of the light globe.

The darkest day for Thomas Carlyle was when his friend John Stuart Mill came to visit and said, "I don't know how to tell you this, but . . . remember the manuscript you gave me to read? Well, the maid used it to light the fire."

Carlyle was first enraged, then grieved. At last a deep melancholy settled over him that was almost impossible for him to shake. Then one day as he sat by his window, he saw bricklayers at work. "It came to me," he said, "that as they laid brick on brick, so could I lay word on word, sentence on sentence."

With that, he began to rewrite *The French Revolution*, a classic that endures to this day as a monument to one man's ability to handle his private storms.

Still when most of us face heartache, our first thought is to cry to the Lord to be saved from it all. We want him to lift it all away. How familiar are these prayers:

"Dear Lord, don't let this happen to me."
Or,
"Let this not be true."

Or,
"Please, please—anything but this."

It is one of life's most sobering lessons that our Father in Heaven, loving as he is, doesn't always remove our heartaches from us. We may pray fervently for sunshine, and the storm still may come. And in the seeming rejection of our prayerful petitions, many retreat to disillusionment. "How can there be a God?" they ask. "If there is, how can he allow me to be in pain?"

A great prophet who was experiencing difficulty and adversity once prayed:

"O God, where art thou? And where is the pavilion that covereth thy hiding place?

"How long shall thy hand be stayed, and thine eye, yea thy pure eye, behold from the eternal heavens the wrongs of thy people and of thy servants, and thine ear be penetrated with their cries?

". . . Let thy hiding place no longer be covered; let thine ear be inclined; let thine heart be softened. . . .

". . . Remember thy suffering saints, O our God; and thy servants will rejoice in thy name forever."

To which the Lord responded:

"My son, peace be unto thy soul; thine adversity and thine afflictions shall be but a small moment; . . . .

"Thou art not yet as Job.

"The Son of man hath descended below them all. Art thou greater than he?" (D&C 121:1–7, 10; 122:8.)

Adversity, then, is a part of the eternal plan. We gain strength and power by overcoming.

A stately tree, growing by a church in a certain city, was nurtured by warm sun and gentle rains.

One day a rough wind blew it over, revealing shallow roots. The tree had had it too good. It had never needed to send down sturdy, steadying roots in search of food or water. Unlike the old mountain cedar, born to wind and sleet, this tree had no need for a tough center and clinging roots.

God's love for us is made of stern stuff. He cannot give us everything we ask for; he cannot help us side-step all suffering, for the result would be fragile souls with shallow roots. He doesn't want us to be whiners, complainers, or tremblers in the closet. We are God's children, and like any loving parent, he cannot be satisfied with us until we have a certain character, a certain nobility. He wants us to become like him.

Then, what can we expect from the Lord when we pray for help in times of crisis? The greatest bounty of all. Sparrows crossing a super highway by hopping may not realize they have the power to rise above the danger coming at them from all sides. So it is with man. God can give us power to face life on lifted wings. He can give us the strength, the silent courage to, like Edison, overcome sickness or humiliation and invent a light bulb. He can give us the steady perseverance so, like Carlyle, we can day by day overcome the deepest melancholy.

As the English pastor Canon Westcott said, "Great occasions do not make heroes or cowards, they simply unveil them to the eyes of men. Silently and imperceptibly, as we wake or sleep, we grow strong or weak; and at last some crisis shows us for what we have become."

Alice Cary reminds us:

I do not think the Providence unkind,
    that gives hard things to this life of ours;

They are the thorns whereby we, travelers blind,
Feel out our flowers.

Learning to love the storm—that may be the greatest secret for triumphant living. To move from the closets where we hide to the front porch where we can see the glory of the sky and feel the strength of the Lord—for it may be as we nobly endure our darkest days that we overcome our terror of the storm.

Remember—there can be no rainbow without a cloud and a storm.

2

Don't Just Stand There— Come In out of the Rain

Hopefully, we can learn to love the storm, to see its benefits and the blessings that often come from it. However, as the old saying goes, "Some people don't have the sense to come in out of the rain."

Now let's put those thoughts into another context. There are countless times in all our lives when "standing out in the rain"—putting up with; having patience, long-suffering, and endurance, even unto the end—are not only virtuous and desirous qualities but also are absolutely necessary and are expected of us by the Lord. Then there are other times when we allow ourselves to suffer either needlessly or long after the time for suffering is appropriate, when we could either have avoided painful situations in the first place or could have tried to change the negatives to positives.

Unfortunately, there are many, of all ages, who, even though the initial causes for negative feelings might have been justifiable, remain in the darkness of the storms of life, continuing to feel hurt, disappointment, guilt, and grief long after healing processes could have been accomplished, who seem to lack the power to recover, the resilience to come back to constructive life, to find solutions, to change directions, to make adjustments, to accept and face life's realities. Like a cut finger or other physical wound that doesn't, for some reason, heal properly, they fail to see the light at the end of the tunnel, or recuperate from injuries and wounds inflicted by the "slings and arrows of outrageous fortune."

It seems to me that the Lord expects us to use wisdom and common sense as we approach both of these types of situations in our lives so that we can learn the difference between loving, accepting, and respecting the storms and allowing ourselves to be frozen or soaked to the skin if we can avoid it.

Life's storms, like weather, can take on many characteristics. Some of us have experienced a tornado or hurricane; others a blizzard or treacherous icy winds. Perhaps it's just continuous rain which eventually creates a flood, not unlike Noah's. In reality, some are called upon to face serious illness or the premature death of a loved one. Others might say the storm is the loss of a job or security or maybe a business failure. Still others face loneliness, school challenges, work assignments, childlessness, the trauma of divorce, or perhaps a child who uses drugs.

Just recently, I sat in counsel with a distraught individual whose storm seemed to be the loss of his youth and the confusion of how to handle middle-age and the future. In the brief moment I had to help this person in his situation, I said, "Do you remember the interview of a great old gentleman on his one hundredth birthday? In response to questions, his reply was simple, 'If I had known I was going to live this long, I would have taken better care of myself.' "

Some of us along the way permit the storms to pound and overtake us.

A few years ago a rather remarkable experience occurred along the eastern shore of Maryland. It involved a great storm in the life of a Dr. McAlister:

"As a young man the doctor had taken as his bride a lovely, charming young woman. He was deeply in love with her, then suddenly she died.

"The shock of her death plunged the young doctor into a deep depression that caused him to totally withdraw from life. He would neither eat nor talk with anyone. He became suicidal, and to protect him from himself, friends had him guarded day and night. Three nurses, serving eight-hour shifts, were his ever-present companions.

"Denied a means of killing himself, the doctor's melancholia deepened. He became an emaciated shell of his former self. He had to be lifted from his chair to his bed and was forced to eat enough to keep him[self] alive. Despite their efforts on his behalf, he hated the three nurses with a passion that was beyond mere contempt.

"As the years went on, a certain resignation seemed to set in. He was biding his time until one day he would have the opportunity to end it all. There was one thing he liked to do: in the summer he was taken to the seashore, where he enjoyed sitting in his wheelchair on a bluff overlooking the ocean.

"On one of these visits he surprised his nurse by suggesting that she go for a swim. 'You can watch me just as well from the water,' he told her.

"The nurse should have suspected what he was up to, but she did not and decided to accept his invitation. As she made her way down to the water, the doctor quietly watched her, then started inching his wheelchair closer to the edge of the bluff, where he would throw himself on the rocks below.

"Just as he reached the edge, he heard the nurse scream. Seized with a sudden cramp, she was drowning. What happened then is a matter of historical record. Without hesitation the doctor stood up, made his way to the water, dived in, and swam out to the floundering nurse. There he gripped her with his right arm and swam back to the shore, where he worked over her, drawing on some inner reservoir of strength, until she revived.

"That was the end of Dr. McAlister's melancholia. In restoring life to the nurse whom he had thought he hated, he lost all desire to die. A few months later he opened his practice again, and thereafter lived a normal life."

Although it took him some time, Dr. McAlister didn't just stand there—he got out of the storm and in the process he discovered what the Lord meant when he taught the principle of finding oneself while losing oneself in serving others. Regardless of our storms, we need to change our direction and discover the rainbows.

I sat on a plane recently and read an advertisement which puts such counsel in perspective. The ad said: "Let go—and grow: To climb, one hand must go above the other—so in life. We succeed not by hanging fearfully to the old but by reaching. Taking new handholds . . . mentally. Accepting, welcoming, adapting new and better ideas. Hold fast, we fail. Let go, we grow. The choice is ours."

Growth and change can be painful. Babies teethe; adolescents have their puberty; young adults have their rendezvous with misery; parents have their teenagers and cost of living; those in midlife have their crises; aches and pains come to the elderly. There is no way around it.

But my, how tragic not to let go of each of those storms in life and get on with living! How foolish to be in a storm and know about rainbows but refuse to see their beauty! It's somewhat like the thought given by Dr. Frederic Loomis in a piece entitled, "The Best Medicine." He wrote:

"It's but little good you'll do, watering last year's crops. Yet that is exactly what I have seen hundreds of my patients doing in the past twenty-five years —watering with freely flowing tears things of the irrevocable past. Not the bittersweet memories of loved ones, which I could understand, but things done which should not have been done, and things left undone which should have been done.

"I am a doctor, not a preacher, but a doctor, too, must try to understand the joys and sorrows of those who come to him. He should without preaching be able to expound the philosophy that one cannot live adequately in the present, nor effectively face the future, when one's thoughts are buried in the past.

"Moaning over what cannot be helped is a confession of futility and of fear, of emotional stagnation —in fact, of selfishness and cowardice."

In other words, when you are in a storm and have a chance to get out, don't just stand there! The process of growth is an ongoing, eternal one. We must continually let go of the past and reach for the future. The man who decided to replant his wife's favorite lilac bushes in order to save them must have understood this fact of life.

Telling about the experience, "he related the painful task of pruning the bushes, preparing the soil in the new location, and, finally, digging up the roots and planting them in the new bed.

"He described his almost daily ritual of weeding, watering, and examining for signs of new life. An absence of fresh growth, he said, made him even more attentive and concerned that he had destroyed his wife's lovely lilacs. The more he thought of his love for his eternal companion, the more feeling he developed for the roots he had nurtured in the earth.

"Finally, early one morning, he was relieved to find green evidence that the roots were alive and growing. He brought his wife to see her lilacs and offered a prayer of thankfulness for the budding results of his work." (Geri Walton, "The Parable of the Lilacs," *Ensign*, October 1987, p. 19.)

Like lilac bushes, we occasionally need to be transplanted.

Victor Hugo illustrated so well the willingness, even of nature, to change direction, to adapt to a new situation, and to do so with a positive outlook.

> Be like the bird, who
> Halting in his flight
> On limb too slight
> Feels it give way beneath him,
> Yet sings
> Knowing he hath wings.
> (*Time for Poetry*, comp. Ruth
> Hill Arbuthnot [Chicago:
> Scott, Foresman, and
> Company, 1952], p. 190.)

Our failures are not planned. We do not deliberately seek unhappiness. But we do sometimes set our hearts on wrong things and seek some things we shouldn't have. We do sometimes pursue the right things in the wrong way. We often take chances or cut corners and ignore the warning sense within us. We are entitled to direction in many ways, and we can have flashes or perceptions that we should live and look for and not ignore. As someone has said, "There is no right way to do a wrong thing." Sometimes we may think we see an acceptable shortcut, but in reality it never could be.

Sometimes we may see others who seem to have found what they want by traveling a wrong road. But if we really believe they have found success, it is simply because we don't know enough. Perhaps we haven't seen the end and we don't have all the answers. We can never be sure that others have what they seem to have.

Rainbows and sunshine come as we focus on positive things. To forget oneself and the accompanying problems, we need to concentrate on others. Terrell Dougan shares an experience of a neighbor's success:

"It was the children who first knew it.

"Now we all know it.

"When Jean Keating moved into our neighborhood, something changed in its whole character. She wasn't like the rest of us; she thought differently about daily life.

"She thought differently about children, first of all.

"When neighbor children rang our doorbells and our own children were gone, we mothers would peer around the door and say, 'The children aren't here right now,' and then hurry and close [the door] again, grateful for the peace and quiet.

"When they rang Jean's doorbell, even though her own children were away, she would open the door and be genuinely delighted to see four or five little kids standing on her doorstep.

" 'My goodness, how nice of you to come see me!' she would say. 'Would you like to come in and sit down? Tell me about your new bike, Scott. And Erica, haven't you had a new haircut? Here, come sit in my living room.'

"For Jean, they weren't children, they were people. Soon our children were ringing her doorbell to discuss their day, their particular problem, and to share their world because she shared hers.

"When we put up fruit, the children would be barred from the kitchen for the day. 'Go on now, this is grownups' work. You'll burn yourself. Don't touch the sterilized bottles! Go on now!'

"But when Jean put up apricots from her trees, the children flocked around as if the Pied Piper lived there.

" 'Oh, thank heavens you're here,' she'd say, 'I've been needing some help. Scott, you pick some more for me into this bucket. Erica, you take the pits out. Sandy, I'll need some help stirring. Hank, you take this money and go to the store for some popsicles for us all. We'll need it after all this work!'

"For the children, she even made losing your teeth a magical experience. When your tooth was loose enough, you got to run down to Mrs. Keating and choose any color thread from a large box of spools she held out for you.

"Then she tied the color of your choice around your tooth, gave a quick, gentle pull, and your tooth was ready for the tooth fairy, placed in its own small plastic bag with your colored thread tied around it.

"One summer she organized a block party, where we blocked off our street and served dinner and had music, and the children sold their arts and crafts. All the people opened their doors and came outside, some neighbors meeting each other for the first time and really getting to know each other.

"We'll probably do it every summer now, because Jean showed us what a pleasant surprise neighbors can be.

"A few weeks ago, Mrs. Keating and her family moved away to North Carolina. The children still can't speak of it.

"She left my small daughter her box of colored threads. And now the children sit on the gutter's edge and watch as someone new comes in to paint the front porch.

"Children are always first to understand a person like that. Now we all see it. There just aren't very many people in the world who love the simple things of everyday life, and who care very much for those next door.

"A whole neighborhood will be less for Jean's leaving."

What a tremendous example of one individual's influence! In contrast I remember reading this thought from an anonymous writer:

> He hadn't time to pen a note.
> He hadn't time to cast a vote.
> He hadn't time to sing a song.
> He hadn't time to right a wrong.
> He hadn't time to love or give.
> He hadn't time to really live.
> From now on he'll have time on end,
> He died today, my "busy friend."

It was Leonardo da Vinci who once said, "You will never have a greater or lesser dominion than that over yourself."

As the clouds of life form and the rains descend, I pray we will not just stand there but will have the sense and courage to seek the shelter. After all, from the protected porch we have a better view of the rainbow.

3

After the Storm Comes the Rainbow

In all of nature one of the most spectacular sights is the appearance of a rainbow following a rainstorm. Throughout the centuries, people have explained the rainbow in various ways. Some have accepted it as a miracle without physical explanation. The Greeks used to imagine that it was a sign from the gods to foretell war or heavy rain. The Norsemen considered the rainbow as a bridge over which the gods passed from earth to their home in the sky. Other men have tried to explain the phenomenon physically—among them Aristotle, who thought that the rainbow was caused by the reflection of the sun's rays off the rain.

The rainbow's correct scientific explanation, here stated in a very abbreviated and simple way, is that it is refraction, or bending, of the sun's rays that causes the unusual sight. When sunlight strikes raindrops in the air, the drops act like prisms and actually separate the white light into seven beautiful colors. There is much more—many more complicated facts not mentioned here that complete the process. If the rain has been heavy, the bow may spread all the way across the sky, its two ends seeming to rest on the earth below.

We often hear the expression ''all the colors of the rainbow,'' which is a way of describing a brilliant display of color. The seven colors that appear in each rainbow are violet, indigo, blue, green, yellow, orange, and red.

We are all aware that there is a legend which suggests that at the end of every rainbow is a ''pot of gold.'' People look but no one ever finds it. Thus, when a man looks for something beyond his reach, he is said to be looking for the pot of gold at the end of the rainbow.

From our scriptures we know that the Hebrews (Israelites) accepted the rainbow as a token from the Lord that there would be no more floods. Following the time of father Adam, the human family had increased, and eventually the people became very wicked. The world became so full of violence and corruption that the Lord told Noah that he planned to send a great flood which would cleanse the earth of all its wickedness. Because of their righteousness, Noah and his family found favor with the Lord, and the Lord commanded them to build a large ark in which they would be safe from the great storm. God also instructed Noah to take pairs of all the animals and birds into the ark with him. Noah did as he was directed. No doubt his neighbors thought he was a little crazy, and they must have made a lot of fun of a man who would build a ship on dry land when there was no proof that a great flood was coming. But Noah had great faith, and he obeyed the Lord.

Soon ''the fountains of the great deep broke open, and the windows of heaven were opened.'' For forty days and nights it rained until all the high mountains under heaven were covered. And the water lifted up the ark, ''and it was lifted up above the earth. And all flesh died that moved upon the earth, both of fowl, and of cattle, and of beast, and of every creeping thing that creepeth upon the earth, and every man,'' except those that were with Noah in the ark (Genesis 7:21).

After many days the rain ceased and the ark finally settled on the top of a mountain. (I feel to add here that when teaching my family, particularly the younger ones, I usually add this verse:

> When Noah sailed the waters blue,
> He had his troubles same as you.
> For forty days he sailed the ark
> Before he found a place to park.)

Sometime later Noah could see that the water had gone down, so he opened a window and released a dove. If any of the ground were dry, the dove would bring back a twig or leaf as evidence that vegetation existed. But the bird came back to the ark and its beak was empty. Noah then knew the land was not yet dry enough for them to leave. A week later he again sent the dove out. This time it returned carrying an olive leaf, so Noah knew it was time to leave (Genesis 8:7–15).

Gradually the whole earth dried. With great gladness and thanksgiving, Noah and his family came out of the ark and released all of the animals. Soon after, he proceeded to build an altar where he offered up a sacrifice of thankgsiving to God for preserving all of their lives. His obedience and faith in following the Lord's counsel had been rewarded. (See Genesis 8:20–22.) Then the Lord caused a rainbow to appear.

''And God said, This is the token of the covenant which I make between me and you and every living creature that is with you, for perpetual generations:

"I do set my bow in the cloud, and it shall be for a token of a covenant between me and the earth.

"And it shall come to pass, when I bring a cloud over the earth, that the bow shall be seen in the cloud:

"And I will remember my covenant, which is between me and you and every living creature of all flesh; and the waters shall no more become a flood to destroy all flesh.

"And the bow shall be in the cloud; and I will look upon it, that I may remember the everlasting covenant between God and every living creature of all flesh that is upon the earth.

"And God said unto Noah, This is the token of the covenant, which I have established between me and all flesh that is upon the earth." (Genesis 9:12–17.)

The rainbow, then, was God's way of reminding his children of his promise that never again would such a great flood occur on the earth.

Today as we live in mortality, each of us has his personal storms and floods. They come in all sorts of packages. Again the Lord promised that if we seek him with a contrite heart and with real intent, he will not forsake us. However, through his prophets he has also indicated:

"To every thing there is a season, and a time to every purpose under the heaven:

"A time to be born, and a time to die; a time to plant, and a time to pluck up that which is planted;

"A time to kill, and a time to heal; a time to break down, and a time to build up;

"A time to weep, and a time to laugh; a time to mourn, and a time to dance;

"A time to cast away stones, and a time to gather stones together; a time to embrace, and a time to refrain from embracing;

"A time to get, and a time to lose; a time to keep, and a time to cast away;

"A time to rend, and a time to sew; a time to keep silence, and a time to speak;

"A time to love, and a time to hate; a time of war, and a time of peace." (Ecclesiastes 3:1–8.)

And in the spirit of that scripture may I be so bold as to add:

"A time to hear the thunder
And a time to ponder silence;
A time to see the storm and
A time to witness the beauty of the rainbow."

I recall reading a bumper sticker one day which read "If you're feeling good—don't worry, it will go away." Probably! The sun gives way to clouds, the storm gathers. It's all a part of life. But there are also rainbows and blue sky ahead.

As the Lord promised Noah: "And the bow shall be in the cloud; and I will look upon it, that I may remember the everlasting covenant" (Genesis 9:16).

As in Noah's case, the Lord has covenanted with us that he will hear and answer our prayers. There is hope and a promise for all. Mark reminds us, "Lord, I believe, help thou my unbelief" (Mark 9:24).

Paul testifies: "But God is faithful, who will not suffer you to be tempted above that ye are able" (1 Corinthians 10:13).

The spirit of that promise can be felt in every rainbow. Remember, rainbows usually do not appear on clear days. They are reserved for the storms and trials of life. They remind us that God is there and that there will always be an end to the tempest. An anonymous writer says:

May You Have—
Enough happiness to keep you sweet,
Enough trials to keep you strong,
Enough sorrow to keep you human,
Enough hope to keep you happy,
Enough failure to keep you humble,
Enough success to keep you eager,
Enough wealth to meet your needs,
Enough enthusiasm to look forward,
Enough friends to give you comfort,
Enough faith to banish depression,
Enough determination to make each day
    better than yesterday.

And it is my desire that we may all have enough storms to give us experience, and enough faith to see the rainbow.

Sarah Hale observed: "O, beautiful rainbow, all woven of light! Heaven surely is open when thou dost appear, and bending above thee the angels draw near, and sing 'The rainbow—the rainbow; the smile of God is here!' "

4

Sweet and Sour

My wife and I enjoy eating out with our family and friends. Like many, we patronize a special Chinese restaurant where the food is particularly delicious and the atmosphere superb. One dish we often order is sweet and sour pork. One evening as I sat enjoying this delicacy, I was suddenly struck with the incongruity of the description, ''sweet and sour.'' I thought, ''How can something be both sweet and sour?''

Since that night I have given my restaurant experience considerable thought. I have discovered that, in fact, almost everything is both sweet and sour—especially life! For instance: We love life when we are young but wonder about its blessings when we get old. We buy a new car but then have to make the monthly payment. We are thrilled with the arrival of the new baby in our home but then must deal with the growing-up years. We land the job we've always wanted and then discover the environment is a disaster area. We receive a compliment and then get a blast of criticism. We can have a great spiritual experience, which is then nullified by daily demands and the mechanics of routine living. It's the ups and then the downs. It rains and thunders followed by a rainbow and sunshine.

Life seems to revolve around extremes and contrasts. A Hindu convert to Christianity, Sadhu Sundar Singh became a missionary in India. His parable gives insight into such experiences:

"One late afternoon Sadhu was traveling on foot through the Himalayas with a Buddhist monk. It was bitter cold, and with night coming on, the monk warned Sadhu that they were in danger of freezing to death if they did not reach the monastery before darkness fell.

"Just as they were traversing a narrow path above a steep precipice, they heard a cry [for] help. Down the cliff lay a man, fallen and badly hurt. The monk looked at Sadhu and said, 'Do not stop. God has brought this man to his fate. He must work it out for himself. Let us hurry on before we, too, perish.'

"But Sadhu, the Christian, replied: 'God has sent me here to help my brother. I cannot abandon him.'

"The monk made off through the whirling snow, while the missionary clambered down. The man's leg was broken and he could not walk. So Sadhu took his blanket, made a sling of it, and tied the man on his back. Then, bending under his burden, he began a body-torturing climb. By the time he reached the narrow path again, he was drenched with perspiration.

"Doggedly, he made his way on through the deepening snow. It was dark now, and it was all he could do to follow the path. But he persevered, and though faint with fatigue and overheated from exertion, he finally saw ahead the lights of the monastery.

"Then, for the first time, Sadhu stumbled and nearly fell. But not from weakness. He had stumbled over some object lying in the road. Slowly he bent down on one knee and brushed the snow off the object. It was the body of the monk, frozen to death.

"Years later a disciple of Sadhu's asked him, 'What is life's most difficult task?'

"Without hesitation Sadhu replied, 'To have no burden to carry.' "

What a great moral! Now, let me ask the question one more time: "What is life's most difficult task?" The answer: "To have no burden to carry."

As the parable pointed out, we are often asked to help carry the burdens of others. Someone who understood what this can do for us has said, "When you are exasperated by interruptions, try to remember that their very frequency may indicate the value of your life. Only the people who are full of help and strength are burdened by other persons' needs. The interruptions which we chafe at are the credentials of our indispensability. The greatest condemnation that anybody could incur—and it is a danger to guard against—is to be so independent, so unhelpful, that nobody ever interrupts us and we are kept comfortably alone."

It's as necessary to have a burden as it is to rest. In fact, why would rest ever be enjoyable at all if we first hadn't carried a burden? Why would sunshine ever be a joy if we hadn't first had to walk in the storm and rain?

The Lord in his wisdom teaches the principle best: "For if they never should have bitter [sour] they could not know the sweet" (D&C 29:39).

One of my favorite Americans, George Washington, understood this principle just about as well as anyone. He understood that when we don't have burdens, we grow lazy and useless. In fact, boredom sets in.

In 1777, Washington and his soldiers faced a cold, bleak winter of inactivity near Morristown, New Jersey. Historians record:

"Washington noticed signs of restlessness and grumbling. Grim-faced, he told the engineering officers that a fort must be built quickly. He had the sentry guard increased.

"Work on the fortifications started on the double. The soldiers snapped out of their lassitude and began guessing when the attack might occur. When spring thaws came, the fort was not quite finished, but the general ordered a move.

" 'But will we move before the fort is finished?' the chief of engineers asked.

" 'It has served its purpose,' Washington replied with a twinkle. 'The fort was just nonsense, to keep the men busy at something they thought important.' "

That fort was known as Fort Nonsense.

Well, it may have been called Fort Nonsense, but Washington knew it was the salvation of his troops that cold winter. Knowing his motives, we might well call the project Fort Common Sense.

Have you noticed that a wise Father in Heaven uses the same reasoning with us as Washington did with his soldiers? Because of law and agency, no one is exempt from burdens. When physical, spiritual, moral, or intellectual laws are broken, there are consequences. Through choices, often made in ignorance, we sometimes experience burdens. We all carry our burdens. In one way or another, we share the load. Adam and Eve had their Cain. Moses needed Aaron to compensate for his weakness. The Apostle Paul had to endure his "thorn in the side."

President Spencer W. Kimball had to speak in a whisper. Christ himself had his Gethsemane and his cross. No one is exempt.

Since we are all "burdened," and since these burdens are as necessary as life itself, and inasmuch as they will inevitably be a part of our mortal existence, it is important that we learn how to carry them. There is a fascinating story of one individual who did learn.

When I was a youngster, Zasu Pitts was one of Hollywood's funniest and most famous comediennes. But throughout her teenage years she carried many burdens. She was quite scrawny and awkward and extremely shy. Her mother, a widow with several children to support, rented rooms to summer tourists who came to their little town of Santa Cruz, California. Zasu helped her with the cooking, scrubbing, and washing.

"No 'chums' ever walked to school with Zasu, for she was the girl from the other side of the tracks, who wore hand-me-downs, and who could *never* give a party. She could join no after-school activities because loyalty demanded she help her mother. . . . The boys sent her comic valentines. They pulled her pigtails and made fun of her name . . . 'Boo-hoo, Za-su . . . monkey face, from a zoo!'

"But no one ever saw tears in her eyes, not even her mother. She walked alone, and she wept alone. But she cried a lot. Few girls were as lonely or out of things.

"Being one of those little girls who dream mighty dreams to escape from the sting of ridicule, Zasu lived in the half-world of illusion. She saw herself in a dotted swiss dress, not the old faded cotton trimmed with rickrack which had been made over from one of her mother's. She saw herself surrounded by admiring chums, and the recipient of lacy valentines from boys. She went home each day, not to the shabby cottage that needed a coat of paint, but to a stately house with iron deer on the lawn.

"The most exciting dream, however, was when she visualized herself upon the platform in the auditorium at the school, dramatically reciting 'The Midnight Ride of Paul Revere.' She heard the applause! Saw herself stepping off the platform with an indifferent shrug of her shoulders. Let them run after her! Let them curry favors! A great tragedienne can pick and choose!

"One afternoon, as Zasu walked home alone, swinging her school books on a long strap, a pebble struck her cheek. Voices rose from behind the fence. 'Boo-hoo, Zasu . . . monkey face from a zoo!'

"A group of girls passing by giggled as boys formed a taunting circle around her. For a moment, Zasu wanted to throw herself upon the ground and sob. Then shades of her Irish ancestors [rushed] to her protection. 'I'll lick every one of you!' she yelled.

" 'Dare you to!'

"Before you could say 'Be a lady,' she had sailed into them, fists and fingernails, good strong teeth and double-soled shoes.

" 'What's going on here?' a voice thundered. It was the Principal of the school!

"In a flash, all the [kids had fled] but Zasu. Her nose bleeding, she looked up at him defiantly. 'I'll do it again! I'll lick every boy in your school if I'm expelled for it!'

" 'I won't expel you,' the Principal said quietly. 'Let's walk over to the horse trough and get the blood off your face.'

"From that day on, Zasu had a friend. At the time, she didn't know how often he had watched a little girl being ridiculed. Nor did she know, until years later, of the concern he felt when she told him about her dreams, stressing the one she longed most to become a reality—doing her 'dramatic piece' on Graduation Day. But he assured her that her name would appear on the program.

"It was a cool summer and not many visitors came to Santa Cruz. The rooms in the Pitts house remained unrented, which meant that on Graduation Day Zasu would have to wear the same old rickrack dress, and not a new dotted swiss her mother had promised to make for her. Yet even this disappointment seemed unimportant as she mounted the platform [to present her reading].

'' 'Please, dear God, make me say it good. Don't let me forget right in the middle.'

"She struck a dramatic pose, her head held high, her long thin arm sweeping a wide arc.

"There was a spontaneous burst of laughter!

'' 'Please, dear God, don't let them laugh at me.'

"On the second try, she dramatically thrust out both arms, her hands swinging loosely on their wrists.

"Even the teachers began to laugh!

'' 'Please, dear God . . .

"Her voice, as she started to recite, rose louder and louder so it could be heard above the other voices that threatened to drown her out. Then suddenly it broke in a thin squeak and trailed off into silence.

"Stunned, she stood on the platform, her face white as a sheet. She bowed stiffly and walked off, dazed, hurt. 'Dear Lord, how could you do this to me?' she asked of heaven fiercely.

'' 'Don't stop!' the audience was calling. 'Finish it. Finish it. It's the funniest thing we've ever heard!'

"The Principal walked hastily to the wings and she felt his arm around her taut shoulders. 'They love you, Zasu!' he told her sternly. 'Go back and finish it.'

" 'They're laughing at me,' she wailed.

" 'They're laughing *with* you. They think you're wonderful. Look here—when has the whole school ever noticed you before—wanted you for something?'

" 'Want me for a laugh! For a clown,' she shrugged.

" 'What's wrong with that?' the Principal challenged. 'Maybe that's your mission in life. Not many of us find our place in life, Zasu. Maybe that's what God intended. And His wisdom is greater than ours!'

"Zasu took a breath. She had asked God for success—the audience was calling for her, whistling for her!

" 'Go on, Zasu,' the Principal urged gently. 'Laughter is the greatest medicine in life. It brings light into darkness. Peace to aching hearts. Riches that money could never buy.'

"His arm tightened around her. 'Laughter,' he whispered, 'is God's hand upon a troubled world.'

"Zasu turned and walked back on stage.

"She finished 'The Midnight Ride of Paul Revere' to such applause as had never been heard before in that school. A coterie of little girls accompanied her home, invited her to all their parties.

" 'Gee, Zasu, you're funny,' the boys said. There was *admiration* in their voices. 'Honest, you're a scream.'

"Smiling, she waved one of her thin hands at them. Then as she walked up the sagging steps into her house, she repeated those words that she was always to remember, and to cherish. 'Laughter is God's hand upon a troubled world.' " (Frances Marion, "My Friend Zasu," in *Faith Made Them*

Champions, ed. Norman Vincent Peale [New York: Prentice Hall, 1954], pp. 27–30.)

The scrawny little "misfit" brought joy and laughter to millions throughout the world. What a great example! She learned, as we all must, that the only burden too heavy is the burden of giving up. Life is truly "sweet and sour." Someone has said, "If you're feeling low, don't despair. The sun has a sinking spell every night, but it comes back up every morning."

May we all understand that the burdens of life are truly our teachers, which truth prepares us for the future.

5

On the Inside

Dr. Seuss, Aesop, Hans Christian Anderson, and Walt Disney have much in common. Their wisdom is sound and very usable. They tell things so simply that even a child can understand. I appreciate that kind of teaching. I enjoy reading these sages and know that the things they write help enlighten my grandchildren and young friends. I have always felt that anything worth sharing should be understandable.

With that in mind, I recently sat and shared a fable with one of my grandchildren. It was entitled "The Farmer and the Stork." It is one of Aesop's and it conveys a great principle. Paraphrasing the story, I said something like this:

A stork of a very simple and trusting nature had been asked by a party of cranes to visit a field that had been newly planted. But the event ended dismally when all of the birds were entangled in the mesh of the farmer's net.

The stork begged the farmer to spare him. "Please let me go," he pleaded. "I belong to the stork family, who you know are honest and are birds of good character. Besides, I did not know the cranes were going to steal."

"You may be a very good bird," answered the farmer, "but I caught you with the thieving cranes, and you will have to share the same punishment with them."

And then that classic statement: Birds of a feather flock together.

In other words, you and I are judged by the company we keep. Now, while that fable contains truth —and, as I explained to my audience of one, we truly are judged by the company we keep—it may be dangerous to judge everyone every time by how they are seen, or the circumstances in which we see them. Randolph Ayre makes the point that "each time we meet a new person or renew an old acquaintance, we almost always make an entry in our mental notebook: He is conceited, selfish, opinionated; or she is nice, but it was certainly inconsiderate of her to make me wait so long."

Perhaps if we knew the facts concerning the man who seems conceited, selfish, and opinionated, or the background of the friend who was late for an appointment, we would form an entirely different judgment. It was Thomas Carlyle who said: "Before we censure a man for seeming what he is not, we should be sure that we know what he is."

An unknown author has penned this wise counsel: "Pray do not find fault with the man that limps . . . or stumbles along the road, unless you have worn the shoes he wears . . . or struggled beneath his load. There may be tacks in his shoes that hurt, though hidden away from view, or the burdens he bears placed on your back . . . might cause you to stumble too.

''Don't sneer at the man who is down today . . . unless you have felt the blow that caused his fall, or felt the pain that only the fallen know. Don't be too hard on the man that sins, or pelt him with words of a stone, unless you are sure, yea, doubly sure, that you have no sins of your own. For you know perhaps if the tempter's voice . . . should whisper as soft to you as it did to him when he went astray, it would cause you to falter too.''

Then it was Dr. Alsaker who reminded us, ''to be lenient in our judgment, because often the mistakes of others would have been ours had we had the opportunity to make them.'' Another anonymous writer counseled: ''Judge not that you be not judged. God, himself, sirs, does not propose to judge man until the end of his days. Why should you and I?''

Our Heavenly Father sees us and judges us for what we are and not merely for what we seem to be. The Lord said to the prophet Samuel when searching to find Israel's new king: ''Look not on his countenance, or on the height of his stature . . . for the Lord seeth not as man seeth; for man looketh on the outward appearance, but the Lord looketh on the heart'' (1 Samuel 16:7).

If God sees in each of us a divine potential, we, then, need to be careful to do the same. I am reminded of the experience a traveler had while visiting a church in Germany. This particular cathedral was famous for its stained glass windows. The exterior was plain, and there was no beauty to be seen in the windows from the outside—there never is. His first look was a disappointment. The guide bade him to go forward and look eastward where the sun was rising. There, a marvelous vision of Jesus in the temple with the learned doctors broke upon him. It was the "Glory of Christ." He was filled with ecstasy. He came and saw different visions as the sun pierced the windows. There are many in the world who see nothing from without. There are some who view things from a different angle, or on a dark day. Those who come and look toward the sun always see the glory of Christ.

In like manner, if we want to see the real person, we must look on the inside and not just outside. Sometimes there is the temptation to see one child in a family and judge the whole family; one teenager and judge all teenagers; one minority person and judge the entire race; one disastrous marriage and judge all marriages. The list has no end. A special friend and longtime associate of mine, Richard L. Evans, has shared this insightful note regarding such action in a movie:

"In a screenplay conversation, one of the characters expressed bitter disillusionment because of the alleged prejudice and unfairness of a judge in whose court a case was being tried. And from this supposed misuse of trust, this disillusioned person condemned the whole system of freedom, and of due process of law, because of what he thought to be the bias and unfair acts of one individual. At this point in the play a wise and seasoned lawyer said in substance, this isn't the fault of the principle, this is merely the opinion of one person. Then, with reference to the judge whom he felt was unfair, he said: 'He's not the fabric, he's the flaw.' " (Richard L. Evans, "The Spoken Word," August 8, 1965.)

How important it is to constantly remind ourselves of that principle! The fabric of the human race is made of satin; but once in a while there comes along a piece of burlap! Yet burlap is still material, and even if it is rough, it deserves to be treated like fabric. Who knows, perhaps with enough refining, it may even become like satin. Still impressed upon my mind from youthful days is a thought I think about whenever the subject of judging is mentioned: "Within the oyster shell uncouth, the purest pearl may hide, and oft you'll find a heart of truth within a rough outside."

I recall the experience of two missionaries riding on their bikes in a small town in Australia. They passed by a man lying face down in the gutter. Their judgment was that he was drunk. But after going a short distance, they returned and found the man to be in an epileptic seizure. He had suffered a broken jaw and was drowning in his own blood. These two young Elders saved his life . . . but barely. They had almost passed him by. One of the missionaries wrote his honest reaction to that incident. His words are sobering:

"With bitter tears coming to my eyes I realized that somewhere, somehow, I had gotten so wrapped up in myself and in the mechanics of missionary work that I had almost forgotten to be a Christian. How many times had I judged and categorized my fellowmen into neat little files with names such as braggart, idiot, loudmouth, Jack Mormon. I felt sick, not because of the thought of the man lying in his own blood or the thought that he might have died, but because I had almost judged him and passed right by." (Morris V. Branson, "Good Samaritan Down Under," *New Era*, December 1976, p. 7.)

My father once taught, "It is an angry or frustrated person who opens his mouth and shuts his eyes." Why not hold our judgment of others and give them a chance to shine? I close this chapter with a verse from James Whitcomb Riley.

When over the fair fame of friend or foe
   The shadow of disgrace shall fall; instead
Of words of blame, or proof of so and so,
   Let something good be said.

Forget not that no fellow-being yet
   May fall so low but love may lift his head;
Even the cheek of shame with tears is wet,
   If something good is said.

No generous heart may vainly turn aside
   In ways of sympathy: no soul so dead
But may awaken strong and glorified,
   If something good is said.

And so I charge ye, by the thorny crown
   And by the cross on which the Savior bled
And by your own soul's fair renown
   Let something good be said.

(*Masterpieces of Religious Verse,* ed. James Dalton Morrison [New York: Harper and Brothers Publishers, 1948], p. 389.)

6

When You Compare Yourself

Most of us have the funny habit of comparing ourselves to others. It may be almost unconscious, but we do it nonetheless. We're almost always aware of those who seem to be doing better than we are. We notice the man or woman who seems to be better respected at the office. We watch with envy the family that seems happier than we are. We notice the better-dressed, the better-looking, the smarter on the one hand, and on the other hand we feel quite puffed up and proud when we've bested someone else.

You may have walked into a room and found yourself thinking this, "There are those Smiths again. Everything goes their way. They have all the breaks. I have bills and problems and headaches. For me, every day presents its new hardship, but look at them—smooth sailing. It's just not fair."

Well, if you've fallen into that habit of comparing yourself to others, it's time to break it, because there is nothing else guaranteed to make you as miserable. At one point, you'll feel deflated and inferior as you look at people who seem better off than you are. Then, at another point, you'll feel proud and complacent as you look at people you think you've bested. Your own sense of self-worth and personal security is on a merry-go-round, constantly at highs and lows depending on who you are with. You've given your personal security to something outside yourself —how others appear to you—and how they appear is a fickle thing, changing with fashion, opinion, and custom.

Let me tell you about an incident I once observed. A young couple got married just as the husband, Bill, was about to enter graduate school. He was seeking his Ph.D. in history, hoping to teach on a university level when he completed his work. It took him four years to obtain his advanced degree—and they were long years. The couple had two children during this time, the husband was always gone to the library, and there never seemed to be enough money to meet their basic needs. During this time, the wife, Amanda, thought, "I can't wait until he graduates and has a real job. I can't wait to buy a new pair of shoes and fix the car and have something besides tuna fish casserole for dinner."

Graduation day finally came for Bill. He had his Ph.D. He sent out 150 letters and resumes to various universities seeking a job. Those were hopeful times. And then—one by one—150 letters of rejection came in the mail, form letters, explaining that the university was very sorry but there were just no openings for someone with his particular qualifications. "Good luck with your future plans," was the closing comment of each.

But for Amanda and Bill it was not a time of good luck or dreams come true. He just could not get a job. He couldn't teach in a high school because the principals all said he was overeducated and would expect too much salary. He couldn't get a job in business because the personnel directors thought his education was not practical enough, and the big dream of teaching in a university seemed further and further away as the days turned into weeks and the weeks turned into months. Finally, Bill took a job in a filling station pumping gas at nights, and the family was poorer than they had ever been in graduate school, when at least they had had the help of student loans.

Amanda watched every day as their situation grew worse. Bills would come and they could not be paid. The first notice, the second notice, the third notice—"You'll be hearing from our lawyers," said one of the creditors. Amanda didn't go grocery shopping for weeks, so the family lived on just the few canned goods they had stored in the back of their cupboard. They turned the heat down so they would not consume fuel, and Bill was unhappy and depressed and hard to live with.

Amanda couldn't help comparing their lot with others, which made it hard to bear. Old friends, neighbors, everyone around them seemed to be doing better. Bill's colleagues from school gradually found jobs until he was the only unemployed one left. Amanda grumbled, "It's not fair. We've worked just as hard as they have. Bill did just as well in school. Why is everything going so well for them and not for us? My husband can't even get a job."

Then one day Amanda decided to walk down the block to meet a neighbor who'd just moved in. She knocked at the door, but it took a few minutes before the neighbor answered. When she did, Amanda saw a young woman about her own age, with two chil-

dren hanging at her skirts. "I'm sorry to take so long
to answer," said the neighbor. "But my husband
needed me."

"Does your husband work nights?" asked Amanda.

"My husband doesn't have a job," said the
woman. "He's got leukemia." Then the neighbor
told Amanda how they had found out a year ago that
her husband had very little time to live. She
described how he had progressively grown weaker
and weaker, his once-strong body ravaged by dis-
ease.

On the walk home, the bitterness which had been
so much a part of Amanda's life began to disappear.
All this time, she had been comparing herself to the
wrong people.

The point of this story is not that you can always
find someone else who is worse off than you, for that
is little comfort when you're hurting. The point is
that comparing yourself to anyone else is a useless
game, designed to make neither winning nor losing
really satisfying.

We are not all alike. Each of us is walking a separate path through this world, one that has been cus-
tomized for our own needs. The Lord knows you and
where you're headed. If you have a burden, it is because you have the back to bear it. If you have a bless-
ing, it is distinctively designed for you. What use is it
to compare yourself to anyone else or long for their
life or their advantages? It will not change things. It
will only make you less able to cope with who you are
and with the challenges presented to you.

Relish your blessings, not because you notice that
somebody else doesn't have them, but because they
are good and delightsome in themselves. Face up to
your problems, face them with courage, not with the

bitterness that says, "Nobody else has to deal with this." And if you must compare, compare yourself only with yourself.

Tagore once said a sad thing, "The song I came to sing," he said, "remains unsung. I have spent my life stringing and unstringing my instrument." The surest way to leave your song unsung is to waste your life in envy or complacency as you compare yourself to others. This is a useless stringing and unstringing exercise. On this day, take hold of your own life. Build the personal security that only comes with being who you are and being glad of it. Be assured that you have infinite worth in the eyes of the Lord, not because you are better or worse than somebody else but rather because you are you. That you may know this I pray.

7

Things As They Are

Some years ago Earl Nightingale, the popular radio philosopher, asked his listeners to take the following test. Why not test yourself on these twenty-three statements? Here they are, true or false:

1. Children of missionaries and ministers are quite apt to be rather wild in their behavior.

2. Lightning never strikes twice in the same place.

3. Darwin maintained that men descended from monkeys.

4. Hair can turn gray overnight.

5. Beautiful girls are inclined to be dumb.

6. Children of brother and sister or first cousins will be mentally defective.

7. Drowning people always come to the surface three times.

8. A receding chin indicates lack of a strong will.

9. Wearing tight hats causes baldness.

10. Character can be determined by the shape of the head and other physical features.

11. Birthmarks result from a mother being frightened while pregnant.

12. Fat people have the best dispositions.

13. Swallowing seeds causes appendicitis.

14. A liar has difficulty looking you directly in the eyes.

15. Long, slender hands indicate an artistic disposition.

16. Men have better brains than women do.

17. Brunettes are not as fickle as blondes.

18. A coated tongue is a sign of illness.

19. Equal environment, education, and opportunity would make all persons equal intellectually.

20. Red-haired people have hot tempers.

21. Children of famous people are seldom successful.

22. The educating of parents will make their children more basically intelligent.

23. You can cause a person to turn around by staring at the back of his head. (Earl Nightingale, ''Our Changing World.'')

Well, how did you do? Did you guess it? All twenty-three statements are false. Even though you and I may have always thought differently, some things are not what they seem. Personally, I still think number four has some truth.

Now, if such statements are false, even if we have always considered some of them to be true, then perhaps there are some other thoughts, experiences, or ideas we think are true that may not be.

Here is a case in point:

''There was in our village a quaint little man who did [a] menial task. His appearance was almost repulsive. His hands were bent and gnarled, and his shoulders were bowed as if he carried a load. But the strangest thing about him was that he never talked. The only sound that left his lips, and this could only

be understood by those who knew him, was the cry
of 'Chimney sweep, chimney sweep!' This man was
Jimmy Drew.

"Jimmy never bothered anyone. He would walk
through the village streets with his bundle of brushes
over his shoulder, calling out his strange cry. If someone accepted his services, he would sweep the chimney and load the soot into a sack that he carried
away. His fee was two shillings, and the transaction
was a silent one, for Jimmy was almost mute.

"Oftimes we boys in the village would make fun
of Jimmy. We would walk behind him hunching up
our shoulders and holding our hands like claws, just
like Jimmy's, and try to imitate his strange cry. But he
didn't seem to mind; he went about his business as if
we were not there.

"One day Jimmy was on our street, and as usual
we proceeded to make fun of him. But it so happened
that on this occasion my father came up behind us
and observed what we were doing. Normally my
father was a gentle man, but now he grasped my arm
and unceremoniously marched me home. He took
me to the big bay window from which we could see
the valley below. He pointed with his finger and said
to me in quite a stern voice, 'Son, do you see the old
Prince of Wales Colliery?'

"Yes, I could see the old colliery; for as long as I
could remember it had been there. The structure
above the deep shaft was still there, but rust and de-
cay were taking their toll.

"The cages that lowered the coal miners down
into the shaft were gone. The shaft itself was covered
with heavy boards and surrounded with a well-
rusted cable. There was something about this old
mine that made you feel uneasy when you were
around it, and once some of us boys pried a board off

the top of the shaft and dropped stones down into the inky blackness. It seemed like we waited for an age until the stones splashed into the water below.

" 'Yes, Father,' I replied. 'I can see the old Prince of Wales.'

" 'Well, listen carefully,' he continued, 'for I want you to always remember what I am going to tell you.'

"Then, in words of soberness, he told me this story. When he was quite a young man, the Prince of Wales Colliery was the pride of the valley. Almost every family in the village had someone who worked there. But one spring day an explosion occurred deep underground, and a fire broke out in the passages where the coal was mined. Rescue teams tried to reach the trapped men, but each time the fire drove them back. So, in a desperate attempt to save the mine, the owners ordered the canal that ran close by to be turned into the mine.

"One hundred and eighty-four men and boys were trapped in the bowels of the earth. Those who were not burned by the explosion were drowned by the water that came pouring in. Hundreds of the villagers gathered around the mine, waiting to see if any were rescued. But as the hours passed, hope turned to despair. The rescue team that went down returned with saddened faces.

" 'No one,' they said, 'could possibly have lived through those awful conditions.'

"Still the villagers waited, for down below in the earth were their loved ones, and they did not wish to return home without them.

"It was when the sun had touched the hilltop and first shadows had settled on the village that it happened. Someone cried out, and a pair of hands could be seen climbing the cables that raised and lowered the cage. Eager hands assisted the man from those awful cables. The flesh was hanging in shreds from his hands, his clothing almost burned from his body. Tenderly they laid him down, and the doctor ministered to him as best he could. The man was near to death, but the courage that caused him to climb from the darkness of the mine to the day above would help him to live again. The man was Jimmy Drew.

"The question on everyone's lips was, 'How could a man live through explosion, fire, and water and then climb those hundreds of feet on a steel cable and still live?'

"That question was never answered, for God in his mercy had closed the mind of Jimmy Drew so that he would never tell of his terrible ordeal. I remember still how my father put his arm around me and pulled me close to him, and together we shed tears." (*New Era*, April 1975, p. 45.)

What a lesson!

Things really are not always as they sometimes appear to be. I wonder how many times in my own life I have looked at people or situations and misjudged them. I would like to think I haven't done that too often. But the temptation is always there. And one of the great problems in not seeing things as they really are is that our expectations are crushed and our faith in ourselves and others is diminished. I remember learning years ago that people tend to throw stones only at the tree which bears fruit.

It reminds me of an incident that occurred in 1785. On a cold winter day a young Scottish farmer was plowing a field when he turned over a mouse nest. Instead of killing the mouse, he stood there watching the helpless creature, realizing how long it had taken the mouse to build this home for its family, and regretting that his plow had destroyed it. That night he wrote a poem about it—unheard of in those days, since it was not a particularly romantic subject.

The poet was Robert Burns and this is an anglicized version of his now-famous poem:

> But, Mouse, thou art not thyself alone,
> In proving foresight may be vain;
> The best-laid schemes o' mice an' men,
>   oft go awry,
> An' leave us nought but grief and pain,
>   for promised joy.

I believe that since "foresight" alone may not save us, even if that foresight is correct, misjudging of others and their circumstances can be devastating to us all.

Those who have participated in athletics have learned many great lessons. One of the most important is that you cannot always be sure of what you see. Try swinging at some ninety-mile-an-hour fast balls that are mixed with sharp curve balls and you have a testimony of the principle. I know some professional athletes who appear to have everything: money, prestige, fame. But that appearance only hides their insecurity, their unhappiness, their loneliness. We have all watched basketball teams look unbeatable one night and see them get blown out of the gym the next. One of my grandsons watched Magic Johnson make an almost impossible pass for the Lakers and thought maybe he could do that himself. But then when the attempt in the backyard was made, there was a different result.

I remember a plaque on the wall of a colleague. Its wisdom speaks loud and clear: "Nothing is impossible for the man who doesn't have to do it." Things really aren't always as they seem!

Now, may I suggest what you and I can do about all this? Since the principle of reality is so broad, let me give a suggestion on how we might improve.

There are a lot of Jimmy Drews around us. They may not be so handicapped or obvious, but they have their problems. In fact, which one of us doesn't? Well, since it is so difficult to judge, why don't we *not*? Someone has observed that, "He is little who belittles others." Or as my father used to say, "It is easier to pull down than build up." Instead of reacting to someone or something as we "think it is," why not delay that judgment indefinitely? It would be a much happier world if we would do such a simple thing. Parents would find that their youth are not really as bad as they seem. And young people would discover that parents are wonderful after all. Families would find an amazing increase in togetherness, neighborhoods would enjoy greater patience, and all of us would be happier with ourselves.

Maybe you and I can't change the world, but we can change the way we look at it. May we do so. May we reserve judgment until we see "things as they really are." We'll be pleased with the results. And so will those around us.

II

Making the Best of a Rainy Day

8

Dear Friend

During the past few decades I have received thousands of letters. Some have come from people I hardly knew—or didn't know at all. Others, from those I knew well—some from family. The letters are all different and interesting as one considers the many lives they represent. One letter that came not long ago really caught my eye because of its simple, direct, and very meaningful salutation which read, "Dear Friend." Now, those two words have probably been used hundreds of times for salutations, but as I looked at them this day their meaning really hit me and the impact was profound—a wonderful, tender, and very satisfying feeling entered my heart. My first thought was of our Lord's comment when addressing those he loved, "Ye are my friends."

I then realized that the feeling of intense satisfaction which I was experiencing was coming from a declaration of friendship for me on the part of the writer, and I always welcome those pleasant feelings. I suggest that we all desire and, in fact, need those feelings. You and I need each other. We really do!

All during our lives and especially when chaos and despair are present, there's nothing quite like a word from a friend to help us feel like going on. Some folks turn to drugs and alcohol for a "pick me up," but such dependency is only a temporary solace for problems. In fact, such action creates even greater problems and frustrations. But think of the power of a friend—a letter, a phone call, a personal word which can lift the weight of depression and bring a silver lining to the day by encouraging us that we are capable of handling things and are not alone.

There are some of us who remember what Gene Autry, the singing cowboy and now owner of the California Angels, used to croon: "I'm back in the saddle again, where a friend is a friend. . . . ''

To repeat myself, we really do need each other. There is a wonderful spirit of reassurance in the love of good friends who care. And at this point we might very well ask ourselves why. We all know we feel comfortable, at ease, and secure with real friends, but it seems to me it would be helpful for us all to understand what makes that happen.

Many over the years have penned their explanation. Elbert Hubbard puts it this way: ''The desire for friendship is strong in every human heart. We crave the companionship of those who can understand. The nostalgia of life presses, we sigh for 'home,' and long for the presence of one who sympathizes with our aspirations, comprehends our hopes, and is able to partake of our joys. A thought is not our own until we impart it to another, and the confessional seems a crying need to every human soul. The desire for sympathy dwells in every human heart.''

Elizabeth Barrett Browning, the poet, once asked Charles Kingsley, the novelist, "What is the secret of your life? Tell me, that I may make mine beautiful also." Thinking a moment, the beloved author replied, "I had a friend."

Those of us who have enjoyed true friendship understand what Kingsley meant. He went on to say:

"A blessed thing it is for any man or woman to have a friend; one human soul whom he can trust utterly; who knows the best and worst of him, and who loves him in spite of all his faults; who will speak the honest truth to him, while the world flatters him to his face, and laughs at him behind his back; who will give him counsel and reproof in the day of prosperity and self-conceit; but again, will comfort and encourage him in the day of difficulty and sorrow, when the world leaves him alone to fight his own battle as he can." Kingsley's explanation reveals the very essence of the relationship. An unknown writer has added: "A friend is someone who knows all about you and likes you anyway."

In E. B. White's *Charlotte's Web*, the marvelous children's book which was made into a Paramount full-length cartoon, Wilbur, the pig, realizes one day that he will be butchered and cries out in the barnyard, "I need a friend." Charlotte, the spider, spinning a web nearby, says, "I'll be your friend." And so she becomes. Throughout the story as she builds faith and confidence in Wilbur, she constantly reminds him, "It's character that counts and you have a very good character."

Wilbur is eventually saved from the slaughterhouse because of Charlotte's ingenius methods of weaving into her web messages about this unusual pig which cause the world to marvel.

As the story closes, Wilbur learns that the time has come for Charlotte to die. With great sadness he in-

quires, "Why have you been my friend?" She
answered, "Because by helping you I have helped
myself." Then Wilbur makes this classic comment,
"It's not often someone comes along that's a true
friend."

Through friendships come, undoubtedly, some of
the most fulfilling, comforting, growth-promoting,
influential, and thus valuable and indeed crucial experiences in our lives—friendships starting with our
own family members, then radiating out to those outside our homes. Because of the importance of these
relationships and because, as Wilbur the pig so aptly
reminds us, they are so hard to come by, wisdom
would dictate that we do all we can to develop them
and keep them strong. We may safely assume that
the succinct statement made by an unknown writer,
"To have a friend, be one," is excellent advice. And
for those of us who have not experienced the inde-
scribable joy of those meaningful associations, this
statement gives us a goal to work toward.

A further example of the importance of friendships—the spirit of togetherness—is given, along
with other valuable and wise counsel, by Reverend
Roger Flughum as he shares his feelings in a recently
circulated article. He writes:

"Most of what I really need to know about how to
live, and what to do, and how to be I learned in kindergarten. Wisdom was not at the top of the grad-
uate-school mountain, but there in the sandbox.

"These are the things I learned: Share everything.
Play fair. Don't hit people. Put things back where you
found them. Clean up your own mess. Don't take
things that aren't yours. Say you're sorry when you
hurt somebody. Wash your hands before you eat.
Live a balanced life. Learn some and think some, and
draw and sing and dance and play and work every
day some.

"Take a nap in the afternoon. When you go out into the world, watch for traffic, *hold hands, and stick together.* Be aware of wonder. Remember the little seed in the plastic cup. The roots go down and the plant goes up, and nobody really knows why, but we are all like that.

"Goldfish and hamsters and white mice and even the little seed in the plastic cup—they all die. So do we.

"And then remember the book about Dick and Jane and the first word you learned, the biggest word of all: look. Everything you need to know is in there somewhere. The golden rule and love and basic sanitation. Ecology and politics and sane living.

"Think of what a better world it would be if we all had cookies and milk about three o'clock every afternoon and then laid down with our blankets for a nap. Or if we had a basic policy in our nation and other nations always to put things back where we found them and cleaned up our own messes. And it is still true, no matter how old you are, when you go out into the world, *it is best to hold hands and stick together.*"

Such a simple formula but so true. It seems to me that holding hands and sticking together would make us all a lot less lonely . . . and a lot happier. The more I have considered that article, the more I have pondered the letter from my friend and the more certain I am that friendship is not just nice . . . it's a necessity! I recall hearing a profound thought one evening as I was discussing ideas about loneliness with an associate. He shared this quote by an unknown author: "We are all passengers on the same ship in a stormy sea. And we owe each other a terrible loyalty."

That statement rings true to me and is not just good advice that if implemented would make us happier, but is an absolute necessity if we are to survive.

We really do need many a "dear friend" if we are to make it through this life with balance.

I return to the letter I referred to earlier. The surprising thing about my correspondent is that I did not really know him. He was simply sending a note to thank me for a piece of writing I had done that was pleasing to him. But in those two short words, "Dear Friend," he had brought a warmth and closeness that caused me to ponder and reflect. One never really knows when he will do or say something that lifts or helps another. I have often felt much responsibility as I have spoken to audiences worldwide. Perhaps such feelings are best expressed in this verse:

> You never know when someone
> May catch a dream from you.
> You never know when a little word
> Or something you may do
> May open up the windows
> Of a mind that seeks the light—
> The way you live may not matter at all
> But you never know, it might.
> And just in case it could be
> That another's life, through you,
> Might possibly change for the better
> With a broader and brighter view,
> It seems it might be worth a try
> At pointing the way to the right—
> Of course, it may not matter at all,
> But then again—it might.
> (Author unknown.)

It is my observation that it not only might happen, it *does*! Consider the scope of your influence. How many are in your family? How many friends do you have? How many acquaintances? How many associates at work, school? How many people will you see during any given day? There are almost countless numbers we encounter daily. What a wonderful opportunity to help, maybe to influence!

As I see different peoples and cultures, I can honestly say that most burdens would be lightened considerably by a smile, a handshake, a pat on the back, a friendly "hello," a comment of concern. Abraham Lincoln was once talking with a woman about how the North must trust the South. She disagreed with him and said that she felt we must destroy our enemies. Lincoln replied: "What, madam? Do I not destroy them when I make them my friends?" We can all do those simple, Christlike acts that will allow individuals to carry their own burdens with greater dignity. Perhaps we need to retrain ourselves to smile, say hello, give a nod of the head, put an arm around the shoulder, pick up the phone, send a letter, give a compliment, share a joke. The list is endless but the actions are not.

An anonymous writer has shared this thought:

> If nobody smiled and nobody cheered
> and nobody helped us along;
> If every man looked after himself
> and good things all went to the strong;
> If nobody cared just a little for you,
> and nobody thought about me,
> And we all stood alone in the battle of life,
> what a dreary old world it would be.
> Life is sweet just because of the friends we have
> made, and the things in common we share;
> We want to live on, not because of ourselves,
> but because of the people who care.
> It's giving and doing for somebody else—
> on that all life's splendor depends;
> And the joy of the world, when you have summed
> it all up, is found in the making of friends.

Let's give it a try! Let's remember to be a friend to everyone. Let's start at home and move from there. Simple, kind acts are what it's about. Let's do it! We need each other.

It is my experience that as we befriend those in our circle of influence, the Lord will include us in his! ''Inasmuch as ye have done it unto one of the least of these my brethren, ye have done it unto me'' (Matthew 25:40).

There are many around us who are anxious for our friendship. May we be wise not to prolong their wait.

9

Recipes

Over the years I have enjoyed watching my wife work with our daughters and our grandchildren in the kitchen. While my wife is a very creative woman when it comes to making tasty dishes and satisfying one's appetite, she will occasionally take a backseat to one of our little ones. When these little chefs come to our home to experiment, I am always amazed at their creativity when it comes to trying a new recipe.

My wife has collected literally hundreds of recipes from her mother, grandmother, and others whom she admires and has them all properly catalogued in special files. Hardly a week passes but what she will try a new one she's heard about or clipped from a newspaper or magazine. Despite this great library of ideas and suggestions, our little gourmets still insist on using their own creations. You can understand then that I smiled recently while reading of two sample recipes from kindergarten children. As you read these recipes, I would suggest that you enjoy their creativity but not plan to include them in any forthcoming meal.

Here's the first:

Steak and Smashed Potatoes and Apple Pie

For Steak: 1 pound of steak with red meat in it
            5 potatoes or 10 pounds
            10 inches of salt
For Gravy: A whole of flour
            6 inches of water
For Pie: 10 inches of dough
            3 apples
            7 pounds of sugar

Put the steak in a flat pan and put it on the stove at 8° (my mother thinks) or 10° (my father thinks) and cook for 4 hours.

Cut up the potatoes and smash them up and cook them in a big pot for the same time.

Then put the dough in a flat silver thing and smash with a potato smasher and then put on some more dough. Put in the oven at 9° or 5 minutes.

Put everything on the table and you could have company.

Serves 4.

And if my sister doesn't eat her carrots, she can't have any pie.

Sound exciting? Here's recipe number two. It is equally as interesting and sounds a little easier to prepare, although I would not recommend it.

Chops

Some chops that are enough to fill up your pan
Fresh salt and pepper
Fresh flour

1 ball of salad lettuce
1 sponge cake with ice cream

Put the chops in the bag and shake them for 5 hours—and the flour too.

Put them in a skillet pan on the biggest black circle on the roof of your stove. Cook them for plenty of time.

Fringe up the lettuce in little heaps in all the bowls.

Go on the porch and bring the high chair and have your supper everybody! Note: But stoves really is dangerous—and you shouldn't go near one till you get married. (Jane G. Martel, *Smashed Potatoes: A Kid's-Eye View of the Kitchen* [New York: Houghton Mifflin, 1974].)

If those two recipes don't whet your appetite, you must be an adult. I will admit, however, that the concluding note on the second recipe—about not going near a stove until married—has probably been heeded by a few brides.

While recipes usually have to do with the culinary arts, there are also many recipes for life. Beulah Squires shares this recipe for encountering human storms.

"The airport terminal was crowded. It was my annual flight. Often as I had made it, the thrill of adventure, of expectancy, was still there, in spite of half-bored anxiety as to how it would come out. I always felt a little afraid. What did this flight hold for me? With mixed emotions I waited for my luggage to be weighed.

" 'Your bags are very much overweight.' The courteous voice was apologetic, almost as if he felt sorry for me.

" 'That's all right.' I smiled at him. 'I'm used to overweight. I'll pay the charges.'

" 'I'm sorry,' he said, 'this time you cannot pay. The flight is crowded. You'll have to reduce your luggage.'

" 'That is impossible, it contains only things with which I always travel.'

" 'It will have to be done,' he said, and shoved my bags toward me. 'The stewardess will help you.'

"Already my bags were being opened and a hand was rummaging through them.

" 'This is quite heavy,' the stewardess said, taking out a big bundle. 'These old traditions have outlived their usefulness. We will throw them away.' Into a large receptacle, marked 'Useless,' went my cherished traditions of other days, which through the years I had so carefully hoarded.

" 'Whatever can this be?' the stewardess was drawing out a big package from the very bottom of the bag. 'I do declare!' she said as she untied the bows of ribbon that I had tried to make attractive. 'It's full of put-offs!'

" 'Put-offs?' I said, quite puzzled.

" 'Yes, put-offs—all the things you meant to do —letters to write, friends to call, cheery words to speak, appreciation to show, flowers to give, and thoughtful attention to bestow. My, my how did you ever accumulate so much?'

"Without waiting for my answer, she tossed the whole package, ribbons and all, into a basket marked 'Too Late,' and picked up another bundle.

" 'This rattles,' she said. 'Must be chips you have carried on your shoulder for a long time.' She tossed them into the open fire, and up in smoke went my pet grievances.

'' 'This is heavy!' The stewardess was holding a brightly colored bottle filled with dark, heavy liquid.

'' 'That,' I said with dignity, 'is my precious bottle of pride. It perfumes my personality. I'll keep it please.' I held out my hand.

'' 'No!' The voice was stern. 'It's odor is obnoxious. I shall break it!' The bottle crashed to the floor, and through my tears I saw its contents ooze away.

'' 'Come,' the voice was kind again. 'Your flight is almost ready. I will help you repack. Here, where you had traditions, we'll tuck in opportunity—it doesn't weigh anything, and fresh supplies are always at hand. New ideas are so wonderful with which to experiment. At the bottom of your bag, where you had put-offs, we'll pack a whole tray of kindnesses, and put them on top for convenience. We'll not bother with fancy bows of excuses—they add to the weight.

'' 'In place of shoulder chips, which must have been very hard and uncomfortable to wear, we will put pads of love and understanding. They give perfect contour to the shoulders. Garments worn over them have a beauty that can never be surpassed.'

''Over the loud speaker came a voice, 'Flight 1989 now loading.'

''I snapped my bag shut.

'' 'I am sorry about the bottle of pride,' the stewardess said. 'It was quite necessary to break it. In its place I will give you this golden vessel of humility. Let its mist surround you and you will walk in an aura of loveliness.'

'' 'Flight 1989, all passengers aboard.'

''The plane lifted, and I was away on my flight of 365 days. Old inhibitions dropped away as the ground receded. I settled into my seat and smiled at fellow passengers. It was going to be a good flight. I was going into it with no excess baggage!'' (*Especially for Mormons*, 1:378–80.)

Aren't those wonderful ingredients? It is also a great recipe for having a smooth flight in a storm. The recipe is simple. In printed form it would appear something like this:

Smooth Sailing
1. Desire to do better
2. Willingness to let go
3. Several cups of courage

Take your desire to do better and combine with your willingness to let go of old habits. Mix the whole thing with several cups of courage.

Allow recipe to stand for 365 days. Serve as needed, especially during thunderstorms.

It is the willingness to let go that is the most difficult part. People find all kinds of courage to do many things but to sever old habits and lighten the load is truly the great challenge. We often cling to our ''excess baggage'' as if we can't survive without it. I know an athlete who is an expert at using the bow and arrow. But in order for the arrow to hit the target, the bow not only has to be stretched but the archer also has to let go of the arrow. There are some people in life who love to hold the bow securely, place the arrow in perfect position, pull back the bow, and never let go.

Sometimes we are like that fabled Armenian peasant named Josef.

''Josef had the finest lamb in all Armenia. Thanks to the shepherd's unflagging care, the lamb had the richest, the longest, and the softest fleece anywhere around. It became so famous across the countryside that it aroused deep envy on the part of some of Josef's more wicked neighbors. So they schemingly banded together and decided to steal it.

"When the shepherd saw them coming, he quickly picked up the precious lamb in his arms, ran to his cabin, and barred the door. In loyal defense of his loved one, he began shooting at the robbers. To throw them off balance, he would shoot first from the west window, and then from the east. Then he would rush back and shoot from the west window again.

"But each time he dashed across the cabin from one window to the other, he tripped and fell over the frightened lamb. So he finally threw open the door, kicked the lamb outside, and went on fighting!"

A word of caution: Before taking the recipe too far, decide what baggage to drop. Don't drop the essentials. Sometime when we are in the middle of a storm throwing off excess baggage, we might throw out the life preserver. Often the very items we need for growth are the things we tend to throw overboard. Consider the following letter to Ann Landers:

"Yesterday was one of those impossible days. My husband was sick in bed with the flu. Any woman will tell you it's easier to have five sick kids than one sick husband. He almost drove me crazy with his complaints and small demands.

"Our oldest boy had to be driven to his music lesson. His sister was late for choir practice. The second boy had a dental appointment and was making excuses to stay home. The youngest son decided to spend the day picking on his three-year-old sister.

"I had run out of milk and oranges and couldn't possibly get to the market before it closed. The basket of unwashed laundry seemed to be leering at me from the corner. There it was, 11:00 P.M., and I was polishing shoes for Sunday.

"As I polished I felt very sorry for myself. After I had put everything away and prepared to switch out the lights, my eyes fell on the row of polished shoes —five pairs of them. Then the thought struck me. What if I lost just one of the dear children who fill those shoes?

"That's the thought I plan to hold from now on. It sure straightened me out in a hurry. Pass it along, will you?" (*Chicago Sun-Times.*)

How important it is for us then to keep things in balance and proper perspective! Remember when developing a formula for successful living that:

1. Recipes are helpful.
2. Directions must be followed.
3. Excess baggage must be dropped.
4. Don't throw away the essentials.
5. Decisions take courage.

The Lord has given us the gospel, which is the recipe for life. May we each have the wisdom to follow the directions and enjoy the eternal banquet.

10

You Can Change Yourself

As a high school student years ago I found academics boring, difficult, and not always applicable to my immediate interests and goals. After several semesters of struggle, one day the principal summoned my parents and me to a meeting in his office. After discussing my academic record, this educator looked at my father and said something to this effect: "Why don't you check Paul out of school and get him a lifetime paper route?" Thanks to a wonderful father and mother, I was not taken out of school but with care and attention was given new directions.

With that little background you will understand my interest in an article which appeared in *This Week* magazine April 1964, entitled "Late Starters." Several examples were given:

1. *Young New Jersey Lad:* Grade school teacher wrote his mother that he should be switched to remedial school because he was inattentive, indolent, and his brain was seriously "addled." Student's name: Thomas Edison.

2. *Son of a Great American Doctor:* Went to medical school but he dreamed of playing second base for the

Boston Red Sox. Nearly signed baseball contract before his father coaxed him back to medicine. Became world's greatest brain surgeon. Ballplayer's name: Dr. Harvey Cushing.

3. *Young Dane Born in 1805 Near Copenhagen:* In early years he [seemingly] wasn't worth the powder to blow him to Helsinki . . . ; nearly [starved] as a ham actor. At age thirty, wrote a book entitled "Eventyr" ("Fairy Tales"). Ham actor's name: Hans Christian Andersen.

4. *French Lad:* Family in despair. All he ever did was go fishing. Never studied science till he was in his twenties. French kid's name: Louis Pasteur.

5. *Littler German:* "Dumkopf," born in 1879. Parents worried that he was seriously stupid because he couldn't speak until he was past three. At twenty he got a job as a grubby little office worker and spent a lot of time scribbling mathematical doodles. At thirty, his doodles caught on in the scientific world. Little dumkopf's name: Albert Einstein.

6. *A Drifter:* Turned down by West Point, he got a job as a soda jerk. Improved his lot at a bottling works. Finally reached the top as a haberdashery salesman. Name: President of the United States, Harry S. Truman.

Such accounts bring to mind William James's observation: "The greatest discovery of my generation is that you can change your circumstances by changing your attitudes of mind." I personally believe mental attitude is more important than mental ability. Yet mental attitude can be more easily developed than mental capacity. In other words, the person *is* his mental attitude—and the attitude can be developed, shaped, and changed.

In the world there are many examples of people who failed again and again before they succeeded. But earlier failure did not deter them. Why? Because they had a healthy mental outlook that refused to be discouraged. I remember hearing an executive say, "It's a common mistake to think of failure as the enemy of success." "Instead," he said, "look on it as a teacher . . . a pretty rugged one, but the best. You can become discouraged by failure—or, you can learn from it." No one has really failed as long as he doesn't lose faith in himself. Faith in yourself can conquer the fear of failure, and help you to look on it as a lesson that will help towards ultimate success. The most successful people are those who, in spite of incredible failures, keep right on going.

In his article on the seeds of greatness, Dennis Waitley reminds us that such seeds are not inherited. "They are attitudes and beliefs we develop." He points out that the most important quality in human life is self-esteem. He says that "fear of rejection is traced to early childhood, from parents, teachers, and friends. Parents and associates often criticize with labels—'Clumsy,' 'Dumb,' 'Ugly,' 'Shape up or ship out.' All those titles put onto individuals can be very devastating. The fear of rejection becomes a fear of change, and such fear translates into a fear of success." The fear of success causes a person to procrastinate the preparation and effort needed for that success.

If you have no deep self-value inside, there is nothing you can give to others. Remember there is a definite reaction in the body as a result of the thoughts and concerns of the mind.

Some years ago, after experiencing seeming tragedy, Elizabeth Bates changed her attitude. She shares her change in an essay entitled, "You Needn't Have Everything to Be Happy." She records:

"In 1951, I became totally blind from an acute attack of glaucoma. I cried while I was in the hospital, but this only made my eyes hurt and didn't help anything. As I thought of my six children, I decided I would never let my blindness hurt them, and I would learn to do everything. I decided to accept my blindness as a challenge, since everyone has problems, and no one has everything.

"It was Saturday morning when I came home from the hospital. The first thing I tried to do was to scrub the kitchen floor. I scrubbed an area and when it felt smooth to my hand, I went on to the next area. There were piles of washing awaiting me. I found that my hands could easily tell the differences between towels, sheets, stockings and shirts. When I had finished washing a load, I piled the damp pieces on my shoulder and walked out into the backyard with my right hand up in the air until I contacted the clothesline. It was easy to hang the clothes on the line.

"Vacuuming is the most difficult task, because I have to go over the whole carpet with my hands to be sure nothing is on the floor that will cause trouble in the vacuum. When I wash dishes, I have to 'see' every part of every dish, glass, kettle, knife, fork and spoon with my hands to check them as I rinse them with hot water. When I cook vegetables, I place the kettle on the ring, and then turn on the heat so I don't burn my hands centering the kettle on the ring. When I bake bread, I tap the bread. If it sounds hollow, I know it is done. Cookies can be tested by taking one out and tasting it.

"I learned braille, and could braille all of my packages and cans, but if the shape, weight, size and aroma didn't identify the food before I opened it, I just preferred to be surprised.

"Until I became blind I never thanked my Heavenly Father for my hands, but now I thank him all day long. As I fix my bed in the morning, I feel the evenness of the sheets and covers on one side, then finish the other side and smooth the top of the bed. When I bring in the mail, the different envelopes tell me that some are commercial, some are personal, and some are advertising. Of course I must wait until someone who is sighted comes along to read the mail. I learned to type fifty years ago and have no difficulty sending out my correspondence. Do you know that these marvelous hands are the pattern for almost all of the mechanical inventions? Hands do a million intricate jobs, yet we rarely stop to appreciate their genius.

"I never thanked Heavenly Father for my eyes until after I became blind. Now I have a deep awareness of the intelligence that could create the human eye. We have a curved windshield (cornea) and every three seconds the eyelid, using a drop of antiseptic fluid from the tear gland, washes the beautiful window. Underneath the cornea is the lens that can make a hundred different adjustments to give clear sight. The colored part of the eye, the iris, is an automatic light adjustment meter. At the back of the eye is the retina, as thin as a razor blade, which has rods and cones that make it possible for us to see in color and in three dimensions.

"A million nerve responses per second carry sight pictures to the brain for interpretation and filing. I am grateful for the brain file, because I can recall beautiful drives through the canyon, and remember how people and myriad things were when I could see. Especially am I grateful for color. If I touch a rose, and someone tells me what color it is, I can visualize it and enjoy its beauty along with the velvet of its petals, its form and its fragrance.

"I appreciate the exquisite design of fruits and vegetables. When I cut an apple in half crosswise, I can still visualize the star design which has a little package for each seed. Each seed has the potential of creating an apple tree. We applaud man-made plastic coverings, but the skin of an apple is not only beautiful, it preserves the food value and eating quality of the apple for months.

"Blindness, although inconvenient, has been interesting. It is a constant challenge to invent ways of doing what needs to be done or what I want to do. Fortunately, I was able to keep on teaching piano, but because I could not read new music, I had to learn new music by listening to it, and I also decided to compose music. I wrote a little song, 'Pioneer Children Sang as They Walked and Walked,' because I know we are all pioneers every day and either we can sing as we walk through the day or we can grouch every step of the way. When the Primary published this song, I was encouraged to write many other children's songs. I wrote 'Book of Mormon Stories' because I am so grateful for America and because I know we were 'given this land if we'll live righteously.' I now have a group of about a hundred of my compositions. I probably never would have composed music if I had been sighted because there are millions of great compositions available on the market today.

"In the New Testament we read that the people brought a blind man to the Savior and asked him who had sinned, this man or his parents, that he was born blind. The Savior replied that neither this man nor his parents had sinned, but that he was born blind to show the glory of God.

"It has been said that in the beginning everything can seem impossible to us. In 1951, I would not have believed that all the living and working and problem-solving that has given me so much pleasure could have been accomplished. I feel that it is a great sin to be unhappy. We can always be happy if we develop our appreciation and gratitude, and remember that problems are only opportunities and that joy will come to those who work through every day and endure to the end." (*Stories That Strengthen*, comp. Lucy Gertsch Thomson [Salt Lake City: Bookcraft, 1975], pp. 4–7.)

Waitley challenges us to: "Fly with the eagles. Don't run around with the turkeys and the Henny-Pennies who are looking up, chanting, 'The sky is falling.' Optimism and realism go together. They are the problem-solving twins."

Pessimism and cynicism are the two worst companions. If you should become depressed, try this experiment. Visit any one of these four places: (1) a children's hospital, (2) a senior citizens' retirement home, (3) the burn ward at a hospital, or (4) a halfway house or prison. If seeing people worse off than you depresses you more, then take the positive approach. A change of pace or scenery can change your outlook.

I close this chapter with the Optimist's Creed:

"Promise yourself to be so strong that nothing can disturb your peace of mind. To talk health, happiness, and prosperity to every person you meet. To make your friends feel that you believe in them. To look at the sunny side of every situation, and make your optimism come true. To think only the best, to work only for the best, and to expect only the best.

"To be just as enthusiastic about the success of others as you are about your own. To forget the mistakes of the past, and press on to the greater achievements of the future.

"To wear a cheerful countenance at all times and give every living creature you meet a smile. To give so much time to the improvement of yourself that you have no time to criticize others. To be too large for worry, too noble for anger, too strong for fear, and too happy to permit the presence of trouble.''

May it be so with each of us every day, that we may truly have the power to change ourselves.

11

We Are What We Are

A small girl came home from school one day. Her mother asked how she had done. "I was the smartest one in the whole class today," she informed her mother.

"Really? What happened?"

"We wrote on the blackboard," said the girl proudly, "and I was the only one in the class who could read my writing."

Now, that's my kind of girl! Positive, confident, realistic, and above all, she obviously was doing the best she could with what she had.

There are others who might have handled the same situation a little differently. Perhaps they might have said: "Well, I wrote on the chalkboard, but the class was so stupid they couldn't read it!" Or, how about this: "I wrote so dumb even my teacher couldn't read it." More often than not, many today use such comments. Too often the spirit of such statements is evident in our own behavior. Either everyone else is dumb, or else we are! Neither is true.

In a more serious vein, the Apostle Paul said essentially the same thing but in different words: "For I am the least of the apostles, that am not meet to be called an apostle, because I persecuted the church of God. But by the grace of God I am what I am." (1 Corinthians 15:9–10.) Those words are some of the most important ever spoken.

Let me paraphrase Paul's statement in the language of many today. Our little schoolgirl friend might have said something like this: "Well, I'm not really good yet, but I'm gonna try." Or, in the words of a teenager: "Okay, so I have some growing up to do, but just wait and see. I'll be awesome before long." Or, in the words of a missionary: "I know what I am and I know what I can become, and I'm glad for both!"

Accepting ourselves for what we currently are is one of life's most important decisions. It's crucial to our progress. Wishing we were something else, or forever regretting what we may or may not have done, won't accomplish anything. The fact is that we are what we are.

Now, what are we? That question is easily answered. Abraham Lincoln said it about as well as it can be said: "It is difficult to make a man miserable when he feels he is worthy of himself and claims kindred with the great God who made him."

We teach children from the time they are able to talk to sing that simple yet sacred strain, "I am a child of God. . . ." And when we at the same time reflect on Paul's words, "I am what I am," we are singing testimony to the fact that in whatever condition or circumstance we find ourselves, we are still (and forever) children of our Heavenly Father. We may be saints or sinners, but we are still his sons and daughters.

Now, with that in mind, let's finish Paul's statement. After indicating his willingness to acknowledge that he "is what he is," he continues: "And his grace which was bestowed upon me was not in vain" (1 Corinthians 15:10).

There it is! We "are what we are," but if we don't improve on that, then the Lord's grace and patience and love may very well be in vain. It's up to us.

Some years ago I read a story which impressed me greatly and which illustrates the principle:

"Steven had been born almost three months early. His twin brother Roger died three hours after birth. Steven spent his first six weeks in an air lock, which is almost like an iron lung. Oxygen was pumped into the air lock to aid breathing, but excessive oxygen caused blindness in Steven.

"As he grew up, music seemed to be Steven's language. He could sing before he could talk. . . . The day he was confirmed a member of the Church, he bore his testimony in fast meeting by playing 'We Thank Thee, O God, for a Prophet.'

"At the age of six, Steven enrolled in the School for the Blind in Ogden, Utah, where he received excellent music instruction on the organ and piano.

"Steven was a First Class Scout and had earned four merit badges toward his Star. As a deacon, he passed the sacrament faithfully for two years. . . . He had earned two Individual Awards and was working on his third. His service hours were earned by working on church landscaping.

"One Sunday evening as Steven's gangly fourteen-year-old legs swung from the organ bench, his feet lightly scraped the foot pedals, making a slight rumble, and his long fingers accidentally touched the keys of the lower manual, causing a little squeal. Slightly embarrassed, he took a moment to insure his proper position on the bench. Then his music engulfed the worshippers. . . . When he finished, most eyes were misty and a good many white handkerchiefs were in evidence. As Steven moved cautiously from the bench, stake president Edgar M. Denney, with a catch in his voice, said, 'Steven, we felt time wouldn't permit hearing both of the solos you had prepared for this meeting. But would you now play your second piece?'

"Steven smiled. He felt his way back to the organ and thrilled his audience with an encore. His music prepared the way for one of the most spiritual ward conferences that ward members can remember." (Dora D. Flack, "Sightless Trilogy," *Improvement Era,* August 1969, pp. 40–41.)

"And his grace which was bestowed upon me was not in vain. . . ."

I think we've all seen those kinds of people. Their understanding of who they are only serves as a catalyst for them to become something even better. And the remarkable thing about many of these people is that so many of them once thought they really weren't worth very much. But when they began to realize not only what they were but also what they could become, they truly were "awesome." Some of those kinds of people live in your midst and in mine.

In fact, in one certain neighborhood a group of boys formed a baseball team. I think we've all seen that happen before. But in this particular group of young men, one was an overweight, clumsy kid that no one really wanted. He struck out and dropped the ball when it was thrown to him. He was slow on the base paths and he couldn't throw the baseball very far at all. The other boys were very blunt. They finally told him, "Why don't you quit? You are ruining our team!" Now, how's that for encouragement?

Well, the boy hung in there and told his team, ''I know I am not a very good player. But I am not going to quit. What I am going to do is make one less mistake each day.'' And so began the long, hard process of becoming a truly great baseball player. His name was Lou Gehrig, legendary iron man of baseball. Lou Gehrig's lifetime batting average was .340, and nearly fifty years after his untimely death, he is still an example of Paul's counsel. Lou Gehrig ''was what he was'' as a boy, but he and the Lord took him from there.

Bob Richards, an Olympic star and a great athlete in his own right, tells of another young man who also learned who he was and what to do about it.

''Mr. Richards had been talking about courage and endurance to an audience in Canada. As he finished, a young man came up to him and said, 'Mr. Richards, I enjoyed your talk. I know what you meant by telling us to finish the fight.'

''Bob Richards thanked the boy and turned to talk to the next person. As he did so, a man standing by Richards said, 'Bob, did you notice that fellow who just spoke to you?'

'' 'Yes,' said Bob Richards, and he turned to look after the young fellow as he walked away. Then he noticed for the first time that one arm of the fellow's jacket hung empty.

'' 'That fellow knows more about courage than I will ever know,' answered Mr. Richards. 'That is only part of the story,' his companion said. 'That boy was one of the best swimmers around here. Then he was in an accident and lost his arm. He didn't spend any time feeling sorry for himself. He just went on swimming. Last week he entered the annual Canadian swimming meet and came in second place in the ten-mile race. He took home the silver medal.'

"I am what I am: and his grace which he bestowed upon me was not in vain."

Well, enough said. Musicians and athletes are not the only ones to succeed. There are thousands upon thousands in every field who have admitted, "I am what I am," and have gone from there: great mothers and fathers, great teachers and businessmen, great bricklayers and plumbers, great lawyers, great teenagers and kids. They all have one important common denominator: they have the courage to see themselves as they really are and then exercise that courage to allow the Lord (and others) to help them become what they can be. In my own life the Lord and my wife and children have all been helping me now for many years. I was "what I was" when they began, and they have made great progress on me ever since.

My prayer for us all is the same as the prayer of the old English weaver: "O God, help me to hold a high opinion of myself."

If you and I can do just that, even while recognizing how far we must yet go, there is nothing we can't do.

It is my promise to all that if we will honestly accept ourselves for what we currently are, and if we will allow the Lord and those around us to help, we will be able to utter the same words as the Apostle Paul: "His grace which was bestowed upon me was not in vain." May that be our happy lot!

12

Searching
for Happiness

Happiness is often thought of as a luxury to be obtained when all the serious work of life is done. When the bills are paid, when the weekend comes, when school is over, when the kids are raised —then we think we'll be happy. But make no mistake —happiness is no luxury. It's the bread and butter of life. In fact, it may be the single most important ingredient any of us can develop in shaping a significant existence. Is that a surprise?

Think about it. Who would we rather have for a parent—a dour old worrier who never takes the grimace off his face or someone with a song on his lips? Which would we rather have for a spouse—a pessimist who walks around waiting for life to cave in or a person with the resilience to face life with a grin? But beyond these more obvious manifestations, happiness gives us personal power to be better, to try harder, to bear up more patiently.

One psychologist who questioned five hundred young men to determine their degree of happiness made the surprising discovery that a person's emotional state even affects his health. "It seems that happy people tend to be ill less often, recover more quickly, even seem to have bones and tissue that heal better. And happy people often seem to age more slowly. They have better color, glossier skins, more erect carriage than their contemporaries who suffer the graying atrophy of depression and anxiety." (June Callwood, *Love, Hate, Fear, Anger, and the Other Lively Emotions* [New York: Doubleday & Co., 1971].)

If you are one of those who still believe that if life is offering you too good a time, you must be doing something wrong, it's time for a change. Happiness is not a wicked extravagance and working to maintain it is not a waste of time.

While John A. Brody was dying of cancer he wrote an article describing his reactions to approaching death. He said that if he should live his life over again he would do just one thing: work for happiness—for himself and others—and work for it ever day. And Robert Louis Stevenson urged his friends to "make happiness a habit." A third writer suggested that happiness is that particular sensation you acquire when you are too busy to be miserable.

But I have seen many people who deny themselves happiness for what they believe is a greater good. They set themselves grimly to the task at hand, whether it's raising the money for the mortgage or rearing the kids, and then wonder where life went when they look back on grim days. Life's greater goods are supposed to bring you happiness, not demand that you forfeit it.

Don Herold was thinking back on his life when he said, "If I had my life to live over, . . . I would relax. I would be sillier than I have been this trip. . . . I would be less hygienic. I would go more places. I would climb more mountains and swim more rivers. I would eat more ice cream and less bran.

"I would have more actual troubles and fewer imaginary troubles. . . .

"If I had my life to live over," Herold said, "I would start barefoot a little earlier in the spring and stay that way a little later in the fall. . . .

"I would fish more. I would go to more circuses. I would go to more dances. I would ride on more merry-go-rounds. . . .

"In a world in which practically everybody else seems to be consecrated to the gravity of the situation, I would rise to glorify the levity of the situation. For I agree with Will Durrant that 'gaiety is wiser than wisdom.' " (Don Herold, "If I Had My Life to Live Over—I'd Pick More Daisies," *Reader's Digest*, October 1953, pp. 71–72.)

Now, we know that life's happiness isn't just tied up in circuses and daisies, but many of us are suffering from a silent ache. We get in bed at night, lie in the darkness, and say to ourselves, "Is this all?" We yearn for happiness, a golden tomorrow, and we may even get caught in the trap that says we'll be happy when our circumstances change. If we can just wait long enough, happiness will surely come. Another day, another job, another house, another friend—we look for happiness outside ourselves, in places where it can never be found.

A Frenchman once said that wise men are happy with trifles, but nothing pleases fools. All wise men, however, have been fools, so there must be a trick to their transformation. How can we learn to be happy where we are, with what we've got—today?

First, we have to understand that happiness is an achievement. No one is just born happy. Happiness is not a gift to the privileged few. People succeed at being happy for the same reasons they succeed at any worthwhile thing—because they have made it happen. Not by acquiring more things, not by manipulating situations to their advantage, not even by taking more time off for vacations, but by working on the source of human happiness—a coherent soul. People are generally happy because they feel good about themselves. They have mustered enough self-respect and self-esteem to weather life's stormy days. And their self-respect is not usually based on imaginary characteristics. They don't fool themselves. Nobody can. They like themselves for good reasons. They see themselves progressing, overcoming bad habits. They try consistently to live up to their worthiest goals. Nothing will make us more unhappy than believing one thing and living another. A happy person is that way because he is unafraid to tackle some occasional self-reconstruction.

Second, a happy person usually has recourse to a well-stocked mind. "The happiest person," said Timothy Dwight, when he was president of Yale University, "is the person who thinks the most interesting thoughts." And William McDougall, a prominent psychologist, had a similar idea. "The richer, the more highly developed, the more completely unified or integrated is the personality, the more capable it is of sustained happiness, in spite of intercurrent pains of all sorts." The question is: Are we truly good company for ourselves? Have we developed interests and therefore learned to be interesting? Do we have a solid basis of understanding with which to judge the events in our world, or are we always looking to somebody else to give us the answer?

And third, those who are happy have learned to celebrate the small events in their lives. They see miracles everywhere. When Admiral Richard E. Byrd believed himself to be dying in the ice of the Ross Barrier, he wrote some thoughts on happiness: ''I realized,'' he said, ''that I had failed to see that the simple, homely, unpretentious things of life are the most important.'' But sometimes we are so hurried and hassled that we don't even see those homely, unpretentious events that could bring us happiness. We look for big things instead, and put our happiness off for some fictional future day. Life, however, has nothing to offer dearer than the kiss of a child, the first bloom of spring, a hot bowl of stew served by loving hands. The truly wise among us look around and find joy where it is.

There are at least three keys to happiness, then. Self-respect, a well-stocked mind, and the ability to make a bouquet of the flowers close at hand. All of these are things over which you have control. You don't have to wait for happiness or look to somebody else to supply your longing. You simply have to make the decision that happiness is what you want—and now.

I close this chapter with twelve simple rules for achieving happiness:

1. Live a simple life. Be temperate in your habits. Avoid self-seeking and selfishness. Make simplicity the keynote of your daily plans. Simple things are best.

2. Spend less than you earn. This may be difficult but it pays big dividends. Keep out of debt. Cultivate frugality, prudence, and self-denial. Avoid extravagance.

3. Think constructively. Train yourself to think clearly and accurately. Fill your mind with useful thoughts. Stand porter at the door of your mind.

4. Cultivate a yielding disposition. Resist the common tendency to want things your own way. Try to see the other person's point of view.

5. Be grateful. Begin the day with gratitude for your opportunities and blessings. Be glad for the privilege of life and work.

6. Rule your moods. Cultivate a mental attitude of peace and goodwill.

7. Give generously. There is no greater joy in life than to render happiness to others by means of intelligent and sincere giving.

8. Work with right motives. The highest purpose of your life should be to grow in spiritual grace and power.

9. Be interested in others. Divert your mind from self-centeredness. To the degree that you give, serve, and help will you experience happiness as a by-product.

10. Live in the daylight compartment. This means living one day at a time. Concentrate on your immediate task. Make the most of today, for it is all that you have.

11. Have a hobby. Nature study, walking, gardening, music, golfing, carpentry, stamp collecting, sketching, voice culture, foreign language, books, photography, social service, public speaking, travel, and authorship are samples. Cultivate an avocation to which you can turn for diversion and relaxation.

12. Keep close to God. True and enduring happiness depends on close alliance with him. It is your privilege to share his thoughts for your spiritual nourishment and to have a constant assurance of divine protection and guidance.

13

The Greatest Victory

A common activity among young people is that of responding to a challenge or a dare. To many, years ago, it might have included a drag race on a busy road or playing "chicken" with motor vehicles. Perhaps today's youth find similar pressures from their peers in drug- or alcohol-related experiments. I recall vividly that as a fourteen-year-old youth I responded to a friend's dare by jumping on a "slow-moving" freight train as it moved through the train yard: I ended up sixty miles away while my mother waited for my arrival at supper. As if that weren't enough, I once took the dare to walk on the handrailing of a bridge that spanned a large river. One slip could have caused serious injury or even death. I am sure many of us could relate similar acts of foolishness and stupidity.

A special friend of mine shared this experience some years ago:

"When I was a young man I lived in a small community close to the mountains. I was a lifeguard and did lots of swimming. We used to go tubing down rivers and all those crazy things that advisers worry about but guys get excited about. We went swimming at a place called East Canyon, a beautiful man-made reservoir. The dam is in a narrow neck of the canyon between sheer rock walls.

"None of us had boats, so we couldn't water ski, but we would do what we called cliff diving. We'd climb up those rocks and dive into the reservoir. We'd always wear tennis shoes because the rocks were so sharp. We used to have a wonderful time. I guess I didn't realize how really dangerous it was.

"After we'd been there several times and pretty well knew the rocks, cliffs, and the water depth, two or three of us hard-core East Canyon divers got into the inevitable teenage contest of raw courage. One guy climbed up to where we always dove from and yelled down, 'Hey! I'll bet I dare dive higher than anybody here!'

" 'Ah, go on!'

"So he climbed up to the top of the dam. The dam was about fifty feet off the water. Diving into the air he arched into the water, and like a bunch of sheep we crawled up the rocks, out onto the dam, and all of us dove off. I don't know if you've ever jumped fifty feet—it's a long way. I could only think that, after all, the water was seventy feet deep and couldn't hurt all that much.

"Well, that didn't satisfy my friend, and so he said, 'All right, I'll do one better!' He climbed sixty feet up the side of the cliff. And not wanting to be outdone, I climbed up by him. After all, everyone was looking at me. I had a great suntan, and I was sure everyone expected me to do what he was doing.

He swallowed hard, buried his fear, and from trembling knees arched his back, and floated through sixty feet of air into the water.

"I was grateful nobody was watching me as I prepared for my dive. When he'd cleared and seemed to be all right, I took courage, and I made my dive. By now the other members of our diving contest had backed down, figuring it was a little high. But not my friend. He climbed on up to about 70 feet and once more prepared to dive. From below I could barely see him. Seventy feet is a very long way up on the rocks. I said to myself, 'I hope he doesn't do it because if *he* does it, then obviously *I've* got to do it, and I really don't want to.' About then I saw a pink body float through the air and splash into the water not far from me. He came up laughing, rubbing his shoulders and his eyes, and said, 'Well, Merrill, are you going to do it?'

"And so I swam back to the shore and climbed up the rocks. I knew I only had the courage for one more jump. I knew if I jumped at seventy feet, he was going to go higher, so I thought, 'Well, I might as well go up to the very top where there is no way he can go higher.'

"I scrambled up eighty feet to the very top of the cliff. As I turned around and looked down, I saw that the cliffs were back away from the water at that height. I had two challenges: to fall eighty feet and to get enough clearance to avoid hitting the rocks at the bottom. Everybody was egging me on in a negative way. 'You're chicken, you're chicken!'

"I stood there all alone, everybody waiting down below. The water was so far away it looked like crinkled tinfoil in the sun. I was just terrified. I was committed, but I had not even based my decision on what I wanted to do or what I felt was right. I had

based it on about a half-dozen guys whose names I
don't even remember who were yelling, 'Hey,
chicken, are you going to do it!'

"I realized that in order to make the jump I would
have to run a distance to get enough momentum to
carry me over the rocks below. So I backed up and
ran as hard as I could toward the edge. I found the
mark I had carefully laid at the edge of the rock and
sprang out into space. I don't know how long it takes
to fall eighty feet, but for me it took about a week. On
the way down I remembered distinctly how my
parents and teachers had taught me to be careful
when making decisions because I could kill myself
with a wrong one. I said to myself, 'You have done it;
you have killed yourself, because when you hit the
water you'll be going so fast that it might as well be
concrete.' And when I hit the water, I was sure it was
concrete. I didn't know how far down you go when
you jump from eighty feet, but I'll tell you, I was a
grateful lad when my head finally popped above
water. I took a quick inventory to make sure that the
throbbing pain in my right thigh didn't designate the
loss of anything important." (Kieth Merrill, "Decid-
ing about Decisions," *New Era*, June 1976, p. 12.)

Sound familiar? I look back on my own life and
shudder as I see what could have resulted from some
of my decisions. I'm certain that many guardian
angels have worked overtime for many of us. It's a lot
like the city boy who went to work on the farm. His
job was to sort potatoes. As he was working one day,
an observer asked how he was doing in his new farm
employment. His reply was a classic. He said, "I like
the work all right, but it's the decisions that get me
down!"

But really that is what life is all about. We make
decisions consciously or unconsciously, but we still

make them—many times every day. As long as we are privileged to be a part of this world, we will be involved in the process of making decisions. I am really grateful for the opportunity!

Since we have this opportunity, we may as well make the best of it. We can often determine whether we stand in the storm or in the sunshine. But, just as sure as we live, key decisions of today will determine in large measure whether there will be a rainbow tomorrow.

I have long enjoyed and appreciated three short classic statements that clarify for me what I mean. The first is by George Moore, the second by Ralph Waldo Emerson, and the third by Phillips Brooks.

"The difficulty with life is the choice" (George Moore, *Bending on the Bough*, Act IV).

"One of the illusions of life is that the present hour is not the critical [or] decisive hour. Write it on your heart that every day is [a decisive] day." (Ralph Waldo Emerson.)

"Some day in the years to come, you will be wrestling with the great temptation, or trembling under the great sorrow of your life. But the real struggle is here, now. . . . Now it is being decided whether, in the day of your supreme sorrow or temptation, you shall miserably fail or gloriously conquer. Character cannot be made except by a steady, long continued process." (Phillips Brooks.)

My plea for us all is to sense, more than ever before, that our decisions today are truly important. If we could pause and think for just a moment before we make those daily choices, we would be much happier in the long run. I firmly believe that there would be fewer storms and more rainbows for every one of us.

I think about my own life as a young man and about certain decisions I made and how the commitments I made and have kept have influenced my life ever since. The effects are still intact. For that, I will be eternally grateful.

I think the great American educator Ivor Griffith summed up such feelings and testimony when he said, "Character is a victory, not a gift."

Without being pessimistic, I do believe life is full of many battles, and that every small and quiet decision we properly make is a victory won. And if you and I would be wise enough to think, ponder, and pray before we decide, our victories would come more often and the consequences would be sweeter. Andrew Jackson said: "Take time to deliberate, but when the time for action arrives, stop thinking and go in."

Think of the many key decisions we make that can and do effect us eternally. Often in tender teenage years we decide who we will date and how seriously. The choice of a marraige partner can literally decide our joy or sorrow for the future. Our education, choice of a profession, where we live, and even our acceptance or rejection of gospel truths will determine how we spend future years.

I remember hearing a wise man say: "When you are facing a dilemma and you are not quite sure which of two decisions to make, apply the test of universality. Suppose your personal decision became a universal custom—would it bring the world happiness or sorrow?" That is a pretty good test. I have found that when I need to make an important decision it is helpful to get away from the crowd and just think. And while pondering what to do I ask hard questions about myself. For example: Am I really the manner of person I think I am? Am I always honest? Am I truthful in all of my dealings? Is my life as good and upright at midnight as it is at noon? Are my attitudes and outlook as good at a ballgame as they might appear at church? Once our thinking is clear and we become honest with ourselves, I find that decision-making is much easier. Sometimes in such personal interviews I discover a need to change my own direction.

Even under the best of circumstances we can occasionally make wrong choices. Who hasn't? But even then we can do our very best in changing or altering situations to make the results more positive. Fortunately, change is a part of growth and development.

It was Madame Chiang Kai-shek, that grand lady of China, who said: "If the past has taught us anything it is that every cause brings its effect, every action has a consequence. This thought, in my opinion, is the moral foundation of the universe; it applies equally in this world and the next.

"Too often it seems that the wicked wax and prosper. But we can say with certitude that, with the individual as with the nation, the flourishing of the wicked is an illusion, for, unceasingly, life keeps books on us all.

"In the end, we are all the sum total of our actions. Character cannot be counterfeited, nor can it be put on and cast off as if it were a garment to meet the whim of the moment. Like the markings on wood which are ingrained in the very heart of the tree, character requires time and nurture for growth and development.

"Thus also, day by day, we write our own destiny; for inexorably we become what we do. This, I believe, is the supreme logic and law of life."

How important, then, is our need to think carefully before we make decisions! Truly our greatest victory comes in making right choices.

III

---

*Light Through
the Clouds*

14

Dear God

We adults get so serious sometimes it is almost frightening. Everything seems critical. Everything must be done now. Everything is a matter of life and death. We get depressed and we think we'll never get out. We're in financial trouble and wait apprehensively for the worst possible outcome. Our children struggle and suffer and we often feel like going to pieces. We don't get the job we desperately wanted and our future seems doomed. Our lives are just not what we think they should be and the world seems to come to an end. In our anguish we cry out to our Heavenly Father. And somehow, as one person noted, instead of comfort, we almost expect to hear his reproving voice say, ''You're lucky to get off this easily!''

Then there is our small counterpart—a child. Pure and innocent, children, because they know so little about the world and its strife, frequently understand and see things in a much more positive way, in a very trusting way—often so differently than do those of us much older and "wiser." They, too, feel; they suffer; they're sad and happy; they're just like we are—and yet they're so much better because they accept things on simple faith. Oh, for the faith of a child!

Isaiah said it best: "And a little child shall lead them" (Isaiah 11:6). Children show us the way. Despite our sophistication and worldly wisdom, we often tend to panic at the slightest hint of stress. But young people somehow manage to keep their heads above water even in a flood. We can learn so much from them, especially about their feelings of what God is really like, and how they manage to keep calm in the storm.

Another thing I'm sure we've all observed about children is their honesty, their painful frankness. Whatever they think, they usually say—they tell it the way it is. I like to call it *realistic* honesty! Over the years I have collected writings of the feelings of young people as they have shared thoughts about life. To me these are "exhibit A" as to why children are so wonderfully resilient. The following choice thoughts have to do with our Heavenly Father and several children's uncanny (and realistic) concepts of him:

> Dear God: I voted for you in this year's all-star game. See:
>   Outfielders—
>   X Dave Winfield
>   X Jim Rice
>   X God
> I didn't know which league to put you in, so I put you in the American. We can't lose with you. Hope it gives you a laugh.
>   —Tommy (age 11)

Now, add this one:

Dear God: Did you make any money on the movie, *Oh God, Book II?* Just kidding.
—Jerome (age 12)

Here's another:

Dear God: We are learning about Jonah and the whale, where he swallowed him and everything. It is the best story I ever heard with action and fright. My daddy says it sounds pretty fishy. Do you think that's funny?
Very truly,
Sidney (age 9)

Imagine! Believing in a God with a sense of humor! Is it possible that our Heavenly Father can smile? Just look at some of us and our situations, and can you doubt it! But most important, what difference would it make to us adults if we believed that, instead of trying to "get us," our Heavenly Father actually loves us and takes joy in watching our progress—day by day, little by little? And when we fall and make outrageous mistakes, wouldn't we feel better about ourselves if we understood that he smiles in love and understanding? The scriptures make it very clear that God cannot tolerate sin, but could it be he really loves the sinner and smiles in compassion even when we can't? Such a concept makes a world of difference in how we approach him—and each other!

Here's another example of a child's simple faith in God's existence and concern for us.

Dear God: My mom says that I can only stay outside after school till it gets dark. My question

is: Can you make the sun stand still? I figured if
you did it once, you could probably do it again.
                              —Freddie (age 11)

Not bad for an eleven-year-old! Let's add one more:

Dear God: My mom is acting weird because she
is getting old. Can you take back a few gray
hairs? That would help bring the house back to
normal. Thanks for what you can do.
                              —Mike (age 9)

Talk about faith! Children don't just *believe* in miracles, they expect them! Why not stop the sun again?
Why not take back "a few gray hairs"? Or, for you
and me, why not expect the Lord to hear our prayers?
to help us through our depression? to give us peace
of mind? to see us through a divorce? a financial crisis? to help us pass the exams?

I submit that childlike faith goes much deeper
than we realize. You and I both know that with our
finite understanding of life and eternity, we cannot
always know what will be best for us, so the phrase
"thy will be done" at the end of our requests in
prayer is important. But why not be like Mike and say
"thanks for what you can do"?

When Abraham was told he and his wife were to
have a child in their old age, Sarah laughed. But they
were rebuked by the Lord with this great counsel: "Is
any thing too hard for the Lord?" (Genesis 18:13).
Certainly, a wise Eternal Father can do anything he
desires in righteousness. However, you and I have a
two-fold problem. First, sometimes we ask for the
wrong things. And second, even when they're right,
we don't really believe he will deliver. But we need to
try! We need to seek his Spirit in order to ask for the
right things, and we need to practice our faith in his

ability to answer. It takes some people a long time to learn, but the results are worth the effort. And remember, he can and does smile as we gain experience.

And right here, as we are identifying our understanding of our Heavenly Father and learning the reality of his love for us, his concern for our progress and success, and his great power to help us, we should recognize that many in the world today have been taught a far different understanding of God's nature. Here, in another letter, is an interesting bit of thinking:

> Dear Ms. God: I believe that you are a woman. In fact I am sure. I think that is why the rivers and sky are so beautiful. If by some fluke you are a boy please do not take it out on me. Boys should not hit girls.
> —Trisha (age 11)

Does that sound a little impudent? Such thinking is understandable in today's world.

This letter brings up something else for us to think about.

> Dear God: I live in a very religious place, but you already know that because you visited. What I want to know is, was New York City a mistake?
> —Love, Jamie (age 8)

There are some of us who have a ready answer for Jamie's question, but that's not the point. The point is: Could it be all right in the sight of God to question him and his ways? Is it appropriate, sometimes, to wonder what is going on in our lives? Those who have some understanding of our Heavenly Father answer with a resounding "yes."

How can we go through life in blind faith and never, ever doubt? It is not only impossible but not expected of us by our Creator. He loves us enough to give us agency and a mind to think. He wants us to use our intelligence. The truly great people of this world—the Einsteins, the Schweitzers, the Helen Kellers, the Joseph Smiths—knew what it was like to question, but they questioned in faith. The pseudo-intellectuals of our world question in order to justify their acts. But I believe that our honest questioning will always have a place in God's sight. Christ himself, in his greatest moment of trial, asked his Father, "My God, my God, why hast thou forsaken me?" (Matthew 27:46.) But, already knowing the divine plan and the purpose for his suffering, he trusted. That's what you and I need to do. It is natural to question, but when we don't understand, we can trust, and in trusting we can discover the meaning of faith.

Carol Lynn Pearson penned a simple little poem which expresses this beautifully:

> Of the Mysteries
> I know only as much of God and the world
> As a creature with two eyes must;
> But what I do understand I love,
> And what I don't understand, I trust.
> (*Beginnings*, 2nd ed. [Salt Lake City: Bookcraft, 1985], p. 79.)

One might well ask where faith does come from, and how is it developed. The Apostle Paul taught: "How then shall they call on him in whom they have not believed? and how shall they believe in him of whom they have not heard? and how shall they hear without a preacher?

"And how shall they preach, except they be sent? as it is written, How beautiful are the feet of them that preach the gospel of peace, and bring glad tidings of good things! . . .

"So then faith cometh by hearing, and hearing by the word of God." (Romans 10:14, 15, 17.)

Joseph Smith further explained that "faith comes by hearing the word of God, through the testimony of the servants of God [and the scriptures]; that testimony is always attended by the Spirit of prophecy and revelation" (*Teachings of the Prophet Joseph Smith*, sel. Joseph Fielding Smith [Salt Lake City: Deseret Book Co., 1938], p. 148).

The Spirit of the Lord always attends the presentation of his words, whether written or oral (D&C 18:34–36).

Faith begins as a small seed and grows larger day by day and year by year as it is nourished, and nourishment is as essential to spiritual growth as it is to physical growth. Ingredients for the proper nourishment of faith include (1) asking for further light and knowledge, (2) seeking for the presence of God by obeying the commandments and keeping all of the covenants we make, (3) knocking at the door of heaven through constant prayer, and (4) giving service to our fellow beings.

Joseph Smith taught that faith is "the principle action and power . . . in all intelligent beings":

"Are you not dependent on your faith, or belief, for the acquisition of all knowledge, wisdom, and intelligence? Would you exert yourselves to obtain wisdom and intelligence, unless you did believe that you could obtain them? Would you have ever sown, if you had not believed that you would reap? Would you have ever planted, if you had not believed that you would gather? Would you have ever asked, unless you had believed that you would receive? Would you have ever sought, unless you had believed that you would have found? Or, would you have ever knocked, unless you had believed that it would have been opened unto you? In a word, is there anything that you would have done, either physical or mental, if you had not previously believed?'' (*Lectures on Faith*, 1:11.)

It is in great part because of faith, then, that one gains the power to accomplish things. And unless a person believes it is possible to do *something*, he will never act to accomplish *anything*. Faith is the power which causes a person to act upon the promises of God. James taught the importance of having unwavering faith when we come to God in prayer: ''If any of you lack wisdom, let him ask of God, that giveth to all men liberally, and upbraideth not; and it shall be given him. But let him ask in faith, nothing wavering. For he that wavereth is like a wave of the sea driven with the wind and tossed.'' (James 1:5–6.)

One of the reasons that faith wavers within individuals is because they lack patience. Often we cease asking when we do not immediately receive. We stop seeking when we don't immediately find; and we stop knocking when we do not have the door opened unto us. We begin to doubt whether what we are doing is effective, and we may even begin to wonder whether God is listening at all. Doubt, then, becomes the culprit, the stumbling block, and believing and trusting are the basics in finding true faith.

Jesus asks Peter this question in Matthew 14:31: ''O thou of little faith, wherefore didst thou doubt?'' And in Matthew 21:21–22 Jesus teaches the principle: ''Jesus answered and said unto them, Verily I say unto you, If ye have faith, and doubt not, ye shall not only do this which is done to the fig tree, but also if ye shall say unto this mountain, Be thou removed, and be thou cast into the sea; it shall be done. And all things, whatsoever ye shall ask in prayer, believing, ye shall receive.''

Now back to some more childlike honesty. Think about this young man's inquiry:

Dear God: My name is Robert. I want a baby brother. My mother said to ask my father; my father said to ask you. Do you think you can do it? Good luck!
—Robert (age 10)

Here's another:

Dear God: What is it like to die? Nobody will tell me. I just want to know. I don't want to do it.
—Love, Mike (age 11)

Such inquiry shows true desire to know life's many challenging questions.

Let me share another observation:

Dear God: I saw the Grand Canyon last summer. Nice piece of work.
—Love, Alan (age 9)

Note as little Ralph speaks eloquently:

Dear God: Thanks for all the food. Pizza was the best idea you had.
—Ralph (age 7)

Because they understand God, children are forever grateful for canyons, pizza, marbles, dolls, hamburgers, moms and dads, picnics, rivers, football, teachers, fishing poles, worms, bikes, and warm beds. They love the Lord and want him to know it.

They are grateful for the smallest kindness, and then they try to return that kindness. What an example! I submit that if we follow their lead, political "summits" will never have to be held and World War III will never have to be thought about.

Now, for one final quote from ten-year-old Celia:

Dear God: Can't you make church more fun? What about having a few videos? Just trying to help.

—Celia (age 10)

If I read her right, Celia is asking for something we all want: Can't religion be a little more simplified and enjoyable? Can't worship be a little more practical? With children it is. Sometimes adults can get in the way.

Well, my testimony of the true gospel of Jesus Christ is that it is practical. God the Father is real. He is our Father! And as any father, he understands us and wants only the best for us. He is a perfected Man of flesh and bone. He understands what it is like to be mortal. He loves us. He smiles. He rejoices in our success. He mourns with us in our struggles. His hand is out. His arms are open.

May we take seriously the honest humor of children. We can learn about our Heavenly Father from them. And, as we kneel to pray to him, may our communication to "Dear God" be as rewarding as theirs. He lives. Of this I testify!

15

A Majority of One

Recently I had one of those interesting challenges that comes to each of us from time to time. The day had been normal in every respect and I was en route home. I took my usual turnoff from the freeway and proceeded toward my goal on a road much less traveled. It was winter and the snow and wind were blowing and the temperature was dropping rapidly. Suddenly, without warning, my car stopped. There I was all alone without help, and my mechanical skills could be compared to those of an athlete called upon to assist a brain surgeon.

As I sat there, the few cars which did pass were in a hurry, and it seemed to me as though they were all related to the passers-by in the parable of the good Samaritan. I smiled, waved, and even tried to look forlorn. All to no avail. The walk home (over six miles) on that cold winter day would have been foolish.

So there I sat, and as I pondered my dilemma, I remembered what I had done many times before in such situations and the counsel I have given to scores of others. I prayed. I said simply, ''Heavenly Father, as thou canst see, I am in need of help, and I know thou art aware. Thou hast taught us to call upon thy holy name in all things and that thou wouldst assist. I ask now in simple faith for direction. Amen.'' Many times I have had that sweet assurance of an answer as I have poured out my heart in my closet, my secret place, or the wilderness. Sitting alone in that car on a lonely road seemed like the wilderness. I had hardly finished when a car pulled up beside me and the driver politely asked if I needed help.

My parents and my wonderful wife have been great examples of using such faith and prayers in the everyday events of life. To many who do not understand such answers to prayers, they seem all too coincidental.

Years ago another experience in prayer was had by Franz Werfel, a German author. ''During World War II this famous author was in trouble with the Nazis. Accordingly, he and his wife fled southward through Germany and into France, hoping to make the Spanish border.

''The Gestapo was one step behind them, and capture meant a concentration camp or worse. Traveling by night along deserted back roads, and across unfamiliar farmland, they finally achieved their destination.

''Spanish officials at the border, however, would not let them cross. Bribes and pleading alike failed —they were turned back.

''Unwilling to give up, they took lodging for the night in the little town in the Pyrenees called Lourdes. They would try again the next day.

"Before retiring for the night, the author took a walk and soon found himself in front of the famous shrine. He paused for a moment, then knelt down and said: 'I do not believe in you—I must be honest and say so. But my danger is great, and in my extremity, on the chance that you might after all be real, I ask your help. See my wife and me safely across the border.'

"He paused, tears in his eyes. 'Do this,' he said, 'and when we reach the United States I will write the story of this place for all the world to read.'

"Having finished his prayer, he returned to his hotel. A strange feeling of peace had come over him. 'We will make it,' he told his wife. 'I don't know how, but we will make it.'

"Within a week Franz Werfel and his wife did cross the border, and less than a month later landed in the United States. The first thing he did, once safe in this country, was to write a book, *The Song of Bernadette*, the story of Lourdes."

Events in our country the past many months have thrust our United States Congress in the limelight. Like you, I have watched several hours of television reports that reviewed the proceedings. Several times Congress has had to take a vote to determine the direction and action it must take. One such vote in the Senate recently was most critical. All that was necessary for passage of the measure was a majority of one. In other words a 51–49 vote carried the proposition.

Whether you are stranded in an automobile, alone in a crowd, fighting a war, or taking part in a close vote in government, I have learned that the Lord and you makes a majority—a majority of *one*!

For a moment, let's look back at an event in Church history. I love history, religious and otherwise. Many will remember that with the influx of hundreds of emigrants from England shortly after 1850, the cost of transporting these converts became too costly. President Brigham Young, in 1856, tried a new experiment to cut down on costs. Light hand-carts, made entirely of wood, were used by some of the Saints to cross the plains. Each company of hand-carts was led by one assigned to direct. In 1856 two handcart companies, one led by James G. Willie and the other led by Edward Martin, were delayed in leaving Iowa and, against wise counsel, decided to cross the plains despite the lateness of the season. Winter arrived early that year and their progress was greatly slowed. As a result, many perished and ex-treme hardships were encountered by those who sur-vived. President David O. McKay, one of my great teachers, told of a certain experience that took place many years later:

" '[According to a class member,] some sharp criticism of the Church and its leaders was being in-dulged in for permitting any company of converts to venture across the plains with no more supplies or protection than a handcart caravan afforded.

" 'An old man in the corner . . . sat silent and lis-tened as long as he could stand it, then he arose and said things that no person who heard him will ever forget. His face was white with emotion, yet he spoke calmly, deliberately, but with great earnestness and sincerity.

" 'In substance [he] said, "I ask you to stop this criticism. You are discussing a matter you know noth-ing about. Cold historic facts mean nothing here, for they give no proper interpretation of the questions in-volved. Mistake to send the Handcart Company out so late in the season? Yes. But I was in that company and my wife was in it and Sister Nellie Unthank

whom you have cited was there, too. We suffered beyond anything you can imagine and many died of ex-
posure and starvation, but did you ever hear a sur-
vivor of that company utter a word of criticism? *Not
one of that company ever apostatized or left the Church, because everyone of us came through with the absolute knowledge that God lives for we became acquainted with him in
our extremities.*

'' ' "I have pulled my handcart when I was so
weak and weary from illness and lack of food that I
could hardly put one foot ahead of the other. I have
looked ahead and seen a patch of sand or a hill slope
and I have said, I can go only that far and there I must
give up, for I cannot pull the load through it. . . . I
have gone on to that sand and when I reached it, the
cart began pushing me. I have looked back many
times to see who was pushing my cart, but my eyes
saw no one. I knew then that the angels of God were
there.

'' ' "Was I sorry that I chose to come by handcart?
No. Neither then nor any minute of my life since. *The
price we paid to become acquainted with God was a privilege to pay, and I am thankful that I was privileged to come
in the Martin Handcart Company."* ' '' (Relief Society
Magazine, January 1948, p. 8.)

What a marvelous testimony! Once more I say that
you and the Lord make a majority—a majority of *one*
—no matter what the circumstances. It makes little
difference who votes or shows opposition against us.
There is no obstacle that cannot be overcome—none!

There are few storms that cannot be tolerated. We
can even find peace in the midst of the conflict. President Spencer W. Kimball said, "They who reach
down into the depths of life where, in the stillness,
the voice of God has been heard, have the stabilizing
power which carries them poised and serene through

the hurricane of difficulties" (*Ensign*, May 1979, p. 6).
The Lord is a majority of one for all of us who allow
him to be.

President Harold B. Lee added his witness when
he said, "Just as a flood-lighted temple is more
beautiful in a severe storm or in a heavy fog, so the
gospel of Jesus Christ is more glorious in times of in-
ward storms and of personal sorrow and tormenting
conflict. When the density of the fog of doubt and un-
certainty and dangers in the way ahead put fear into
our hearts, God's eternal light of gospel truth is more
beautiful than ever before because of our greater
need." (Conference Report, April 1965.)

Christ said: "I am the bread of life: he that cometh
to me shall never hunger" (John 6:35). We need to
partake of that bread; in fact, we must take advantage
of the whole loaf and not just settle for the crumbs.

Have you ever heard the phrase, "He's for the
birds"? That phrase was coined possibly as a result of
a loaf of bread that fell from a bakery truck. As the
loaf hit the pavement a crumb broke off. Three tiny
sparrows swooped down on the broken crumb and
began fighting over it. One bird finally succeeded in
flying away with the crumb, the other two in close
pursuit. A series of frantic aerial maneuvers followed
until the crumb was finally devoured by one of the
birds. The rest of the loaf was left untouched. Maybe
the phrase now takes on greater meaning. I am convinced that there are some who willingly settle for
crumbs when they could enjoy the whole loaf.

Applied to life, there are those of us who become
so caught up in the routine of our lives in the Church
or otherwise that we fail to pause and truly ponder
our relationship with the Lord. Daily we need to find
ways of including him in our decisions and concerns.
It is so easy just to follow the crowd. It is always the
line of least resistance.

The story is told of a highway patrolman who got a call that three men in a camper were suspected narcotics runners. He stopped them, ordered them out, and had them place their hands high over their heads on the side of the camper in a spread-eagle stance.

Just then another man in a camper came along. He saw the three men leaning against the first camper, pulled over, quickly jumped out, and ran over to them.

Wanting to help, he assumed the same position against the side of the camper as the other three, then turned to the highway patrolman and asked, "Why is she falling?"

While we can learn from others, we do not need to be just like everyone else spiritually. We can be ourselves. The Lord knows us and can call you and me by name. As our wonderful eyewitness in the Martin Handcart Company testified: "Everyone of us came through with the absolute knowledge that God lives for we became acquainted with him in our extremities. . . . The price we paid to become acquainted with God was a privilege to pay."

With such understanding and attitudes we can weather any storm or crisis. John reminds us: "And this is life eternal, that they might know thee the only true God, and Jesus Christ, whom thou hast sent" (John 17:3). When we know them our faith will grow and become sufficient. To assist the process let us:

1. Make our prayers more spontaneous and sincere. No challenge is too great or small for the Lord.

2. Develop our reading and study of the scriptures to a deeper level of understanding.

3. Make our repentance more thorough and complete.

4. Ponder more thoughtfully as we partake of the sacrament and renew our covenants.

5. Make our daily living of the "routine" be less ritualistic and more genuine.

May we be wise in making the Lord our constant companion; if we will, I promise no power on this earth will prevail against us. Together with him we will be a majority of *one*!

16

The Lord and the Lonely

''All the lonely people. Where do they all come from?'' Those were lyrics from a famous song of the sixties, lyrics that suggest that even though we live in a world where you can't find enough parking spots for the crowds of people wanting one, many among us are lonely. Who are they, anyway? You know them.

They are the family who just moved into your neighborhood, leaving behind a lifetime of shared experiences with friends to become the strangers on your block. Who are the lonely? She's the widow living alone and yearning for the voice or the touch that no other could ever duplicate. He's the Laotian refugee torn from his country and thrust into a new land where he can't speak the language well enough to even ask directions. She's the single parent who doesn't fit the ''family norm.'' He's the young bachelor who, for various reasons, has never married. She's the divorcee who, through no fault of her own, finds that her role and acceptance in society have changed. And we may each be lonely, even amidst a throng of family and friends, when we have thoughts no one else can quite understand. Who are the lonely people? They are all of us at one time or another in our lives; they are all of us, locked inside our skins and seemingly forever divided from our fellows by the boundaries of being separate selves.

Sometimes loneliness can be acute, resulting in loss of incentive, lack of confidence, and overall depression. When we're that lonely, we have the notion that everybody else feels secure and surrounded by love. Everybody else has friends, has soulmates, everybody, that is, but us. But that simply isn't so. And, instead of wishing we could be one of them, it is best to simply deal with the circumstances as they are. We can't move back to our old neighborhood, call back a lost loved one from the grave, or put an ad in the paper for friends. But what we can do is take whatever condition we find ourselves in and make the best of it. We have the power to act upon our world instead of always letting it act upon us. Whatever the circumstance we find ourselves in, it is ours and we must make something of it.

Now, here's some practical advice for handling the lonely days. First of all you can reach out to others instead of sitting in the corner and hoping someone will reach out to you. Very consciously choose someone to befriend. Make a call and say hello. Notice a good thing that someone else has done and comment on it. Write a note just telling someone you appreciate them. All these things are easy to do. They are small things, really just trifles, but like the small chips a sculptor makes with his chisel to create a work of art, so you can make a dull, shapeless day into something special. Reach out through your lonely, invisible barrier and touch someone who needs it.

Second, understand that when you are lonely, Sundays and holidays are the most difficult days of all. Everybody seems to have so much to do. They are busy with celebration, and you may feel dismally left out. Plan ahead for these times. Make sure you have something to do so that a day doesn't dawn with the distant sounds of a parade floating through your window while you huddle up against yourself in despair. You get involved. You plan something. You be a part of the reasons to celebrate life.

But, most important of all, for the lonely days, we must remember that however friendless we may feel, there is someone who loves us. There is someone who doesn't think our worries are trivial, our thoughts absurd. In a world where we seem ultimately all alone, where we feel pain quite singularly, where we die all by ourselves, in this kind of world there is still someone who can crash through all the barriers that divide us from others and dwell with us in our deepest parts. This someone is the Lord.

Who can understand the plight of loneliness as much as the Lord himself? Jesus Christ, despite his loyal following, must have been the loneliest man who ever walked the earth.

Think about it. Who was there on earth for him to identify with? His Father was divine and his mission was imponderable—to take upon himself the very sins of all the earth. Who could understand such a task? Who could he talk to about his quiet fears as his life took him with every step closer to the garden of Gethsemane and the heavy burden there? Even his Apostles could not really understand him or his special gifts. When he stilled the troubled waters of Galilee they marveled and said, ''What manner of man is this?'' (Matthew 8:27). Even one of his chosen

Twelve, Judas Iscariot, someone who had seen him sleep and eat and weep with compassion for the masses, thought and understood so little of him as to betray him to his bitterest enemies. Can there be a more lonely speech than Jesus gave to Peter after he had instructed his disciple to watch with him in the Garden of Gethsemane while he, Christ, atoned for mankind's sins? Peter fell asleep and a saddened Christ said, "What, could ye not watch with me one hour?" (Matthew 26:41.)

But if his friends did not understand him, the people that he came to teach were worse. In Matthew, we learn that after he had cast the devils into the swine, "The whole city came out to meet Jesus: And when they saw him, they besought him that he would depart out of their coasts" (Matthew 8:34). Apparently his act of compassion had been misunderstood, and the message from the people was a clear one: "Keep out. You're not wanted here."

But rejection was not enough. The Pharisees sat in council trying to discover ways to destroy him. They sought to trip him with questions that would expose him as a fraud. They belittled the company he kept: "Why eateth your master with publicans and sinners?" Their voices were petty and biting.

His short mission here was to teach the people of eternal things, but his message went largely unheeded in his own lifetime. He lamented in saddened, lonely tones: "O Jerusalem, Jerusalem, thou that killest the prophets, and stonest them which are sent unto thee, how often would I have gathered thy children together, even as a hen gathereth her chickens under her wings, and ye would not!" (Matthew 24:37.)

And finally, though he had spent a lifetime healing the lame, the blind, the halt, the maimed, when it came time for him to face the walk to Golgotha, he carried his own cross. Where were they then, the hundreds he had helped? History doesn't tell us.

So in your lonely hours, and you will have them, remember that you have a friend who has good reason to understand most poignantly your unhappy solitude. The Lord understands loneliness. If you call on him, he will be there as your companion, to still the uneasy voice in your heart. He will show you the source of your own strength. You have the power within you to conquer loneliness. And, if you are one of those for whom loneliness is not now a problem, look around to find someone for whom it is. Maybe someone else will do the same for you when you face your lonely hour.

17

Find Yourself by Giving

A wise man once said: "We have been given two hands—one to receive with and the other [with which] to give. We are not cisterns made for hoarding; we are channels made for sharing."

For many, these are troubled times. The world is full of strife and heartache. People everywhere seek peace of mind and heart and wish desperately they could discover something that would lift the stormy clouds of gloom and fear that depress them. What might that something be that would bring the much-sought peace? The Savior had the answer. He taught that if a person wants to find himself he must lose himself in the service of others. Developing a sincere interest in and concern for others and then imple-menting that concern in helpful, supportive ways brings not only joy and a great lift to those we serve but to ourselves as well, also making it possible to forget or at least take the heavy emphasis off ourselves and our own anxieties and problems. From my own experience I have found this formula to work almost like magic. Not that all problems and reasons for worry disappear, but if one's thoughts and time are filled with positives there isn't as much room for negatives, attitudes are more easily changed, and the world often takes on a brighter look.

A very helpful suggestion for putting this principle of unselfish service into effect appeared several years ago in the little magazine *Guideposts* in a wonderful article entitled "Try Giving Yourself." In it the author tells us that gracious giving requires no special talent nor large amounts of money but is the heart and head acting together expressing our real feelings.

We also get help from an oft-quoted statement of Emerson's which says, "The only gift is a portion of thyself." To plan the gift of yourself takes cleverness. It also takes a little more thought than you might ordinarily use, and far less dependency on the dollar. A little girl, whose pennies did not add up to enough to buy what she considered a suitable present for her mother, gave her several small boxes tied with bright ribbons. Inside each were slips of paper on which the child had printed, "Good for two flower-bed weedings," "Good for three batches of cookies for your club meeting," "Good for two floor scrubbings." She had never read Emerson, but unconsciously she put a large part of her small self into her gift.

Imagination is the chief ingredient—just as it was in the wedding present a young bride received from an older woman. With the gift went a note: "Do not open till you and your husband have had your first tiff." Months later that day came, and she remembered the package. In it she found a file box filled with her friend's favorite recipes and accompanied by a note: "You will catch more flies with honey than with vinegar." It was a wise woman who gave of her experience with her gift.

Many years ago one of the most famous and popular clowns in America was a man by the name of Bob Sherwood. Near the end of his career he was invited to talk to a New York City church Sunday School class. His hair was now snow white and he enjoyed dressing in white, also, as Mark Twain did.

After amusing several hundred youngsters, he said: "I want to tell you a story. Once our circus was to perform in West Branch, Iowa. When it came time to eat, we were some hours from town, traveling overland, so we stopped and asked a farmer for permission to eat our lunch in his field. He granted us permission and I went to the kitchen of the farmhouse to get some water. While there I saw a small boy crying. He had the measles and said he couldn't go to town the next day to see the circus. Well, soon after we had finished our lunch, we started on to West Branch when we learned to our surprise that we would not be allowed to perform there. One strong faction in the town opposed circuses. We decided, therefore, to go back to the farm, and we arranged to put on our show in the field where we had camped to eat earlier. After setting up our tents and apparatus, we fixed things so the boy with the measles could see the circus."

Many years passed. Then one day Bob Sherwood received a letter dated August 1929. It read: "Dear Bob: Thank you for the books. Glad to hear from you again. Come and see me when next in Washington. Faithfully, Herbert Hoover, President, the boy with the freckles and measles." Such impacts are a part of giving oneself.

A clergyman soliciting for a worthy cause was turned down by a well-to-do businessman with a curt letter which ended, ''As far as I can see, this Christmas business is one continuous give, give, give.'' The clergyman wrote back, ''Thank you for the best definition of the Christian life I have ever heard.''

Probably no gift ever thrilled a doctor more than a letter he received out of the blue from a young lady on her birthday. ''Dear Doctor: Fourteen years ago you brought me into this world. I want to thank you, for I have enjoyed every minute of it.''

All gifts that contain a portion of self say that someone has been thinking of us. It must have been a thrill for one sailor's mother when she opened a special gift from her son. When he had bought the most expensive engagement ring at the PX store where he was stationed, the clerk had asked him if he expected to get married soon. The sailor replied, ''No, this is for my mother. She never owned a diamond in her life—and she had a lot of trouble bringing me up.''

Money can be a touchy gift, especially when you know the person needs it. A young man realized that his visit with a retired couple of limited means could not help but put a dent in their budget. Offering to share food expenses was out of the question. So with his thank-you note, the guest included a twenty-dollar bill and added, ''I happened to run across this fine miniature of Andrew Jackson and thought you might like to add it to your collection.'' The response came back, ''We thank you for that reproduction of the Jackson engraving. It has been a long time since we have had the pleasure of viewing such a beautiful work of art. Bless you.''

Good humor is a very effective way of giving yourself, particularly when handling difficult situations in troubled lives. Humor is often the best way to smooth life's rough encounters. I remember the experience of a man who had had quite an argument with his wife as she drove him to the airport. Once airborne, he felt miserable, and he knew she did, too. Two hours after she returned home, she received a long-distance phone call. The operator said, "I have a person-to-person call from I. A. Pologize. That's spelled 'P' as in . . ." In a twinkling, the whole day changed from grim to lovely, at both ends of the wire.

Humor can often be more than a laughing matter. Some believe, for instance, that next to the heroic British Royal Air Force, British humor did the most to fend off a German takeover in World War II. One sample: The famous story of the woman who was finally extracted from the rubble of her house during the London blitz. When asked, "Where is your husband?" she brushed brick dust off her head and arms and answered, "Fighting in Libya, the coward!"

And, very similarly, whenever we Americans start taking ourselves a bit too seriously, a grassroots humor seems to rise and throw banana peels in our path. It was Mark Twain who deflated the pompous with his remark, "Man was made at the end of the week's work, when God was tired."

Will Rogers, the great humorist, enjoyed taking politicians down a peg: "The oldest boy became a Congressman, and the second son turned out no good, too." Bill Mauldin, needling Army officers: In his cartoon one Second Lieutenant is speaking to another as they observe a beautiful sunset: "Is there one for enlisted men, too?"

Someone has said: "If men behaved after marriage as they do during their engagements, there wouldn't be half as many divorces—but there would be twice as many bankruptcies." Another said, "If a man can see both sides of a problem, you know that none of his money is tied up in it." During a recent illness I recalled what Earl Wilson had said: "Get well cards have become so humorous that if you don't get sick, you are missing half the fun!"

Every day there are opportunities to give a part of ourselves to someone who needs it. It may be no more than a kind word or a letter written at the right time. It may be only a hand clasp. The important thing about any gift is the amount of yourself you put into it. May we all find those occasions when we can share and give of ourselves in lifting the burdens of others.

18

Spiritual Senses

One of nature's most fascinating secrets involves the migration of birds. How is it that a tiny bird, no more than four inches long, can, without stopping, find its way across thousands of miles of water to its destination? What guides it across all those unmarked miles of ocean?

A few years ago, the *National Geographic* pointed out that the blackpoll warbler lives in northern forests, but in the fall makes an incredible nonstop journey over 2,300 miles of water in eighty-six hours. To find favorable winds the birds may fly as high as 21,000 feet through oxygen-starved air. To put it in our terms, we might compare it to a man or woman running four-minute miles continuously for eighty hours! This, from a bird that weighs not much more than a fifty-cent piece.

And the Arctic tern every year migrates 12,500 miles from the Arctic Circle to an area near the Antarctic. Such an outburst of energy, especially on the nonstop flights of certain birds, is almost incomprehensible to us. But, perhaps, even more surprising is the observation that many birds go back to the exact location where they were the year before, some even to the same tree. How do they find their way?

Recent experiments have determined that birds use both the sun and the stars for navigation, but that doesn't tell us enough, for even if they are displaced hundreds of miles from where they want to go, they will end up at the right place. So a German husband-and-wife team put together an experiment to see if by chance birds might have some kind of extra sense that we don't understand that helps them to respond to the magnetic field of the earth. Wolfgang and Roswitha Wiltschoko put robins in a featureless cage and blocked out the sky. The birds, restless and ready for migration, faced the proper direction even though they apparently had nothing to guide them. As the *National Geographic* noted, "The Wiltschokos then surrounded the cage with Helmholtz coils which produce a magnetic field when an electric current passes through them. When these coils altered the direction of the normal magnetic field surrounding the cage, for example, by changing magnetic north to coincide with geographic east, the birds changed their direction. Apparently they responded to a magnetic field and read direction from it."

"What is the extra sense in birds that makes them aware of magnetic fields, when we are totally numb to them? And that doesn't seem to be their only extra ability. Researchers have found that pigeons can see polarized and ultraviolet light. They can hear infrasound and ultralow frequencies of long wavelength that carry vast distances through the atmosphere. Thus, it seems, a bird flying high above the Mississippi Valley might hear a thunderstorm above the

Rockies, or an aroused surf lashing Cape Hatteras, or even the rhythmic pulse of the ionosphere,'' suggests the magazine. Apparently, says Cornell's Stephen Emlen, ''They are hearing, seeing, and sensing a world expanded from ours.'' (Allan C. Fisher, Jr., ''Mysteries of Bird Migration,'' *National Geographic*, August 1979, pp. 154–93.)

Incredible! Think of all the messages our senses aren't picking up. We live in a world far more fascinating and varied than we even dream, but there is so much we can't hear or see or sense. It's funny, too, because we have been so conditioned to believe that man is the full measure of all things that we tend to think that all other creatures only see and hear and sense what we do. There are thousands of stimuli bombarding us constantly that we never pick up. We are dead to them. Think of what we can't see or feel or hear that actually exists. Radio waves. Signals from outer space. High pitches. It's intriguing.

But most of us are interesting, egocentric types. We are somehow convinced that if we don't see or feel or hear something ourselves that it doesn't exist. I think that must be the case for those who are convinced that God does not exist or no longer speaks to man. If people haven't trained themselves to hear the quiet voice of the Spirit, they are easily duped into believing the Spirit simply doesn't speak to them. Because their ability to hear the Spirit is turned off or tuned out, they would deny that anyone else can hear. Can you imagine such self-centeredness?

A brilliant, young Harvard student mentioned that she had been an athiest all her life. And all the arguments for the existence of God could not change her mind. She could easily argue everyone away, but one thought finally made her question her stand on the Lord. ''What if,'' she said to herself, ''what if he exists and I have not learned to recognize his messages to me. What if I have trained my senses to exclude him?'' It's a sobering thought.

A birdwatcher can pick out the particular strains of a particular species of bird, while his friend sitting by him in the woods hears only distant noise. A mother can hear her child crying two floors away in a home while her visitors chat idly on, hearing nothing. We hear what we have learned to hear. During the war, my senses as an infantry soldier were developed to a point that I could hear an enemy's footsteps many yards away in the jungle. We sense what we have learned to sense. And what a pity it would be to go a lifetime without sensing the presence of the Lord and his constant care for us as he expresses it through the Holy Ghost!

Now, just as our migrating birds have special sensitivities that help them travel thousands of miles to an unmarked destination, so do we need to develop sensitivities to guide us through this sometimes unmarked and chaotic journey we call life. We need to learn how to listen when the Lord speaks to us.

I am struck with the incident recorded in the Bible in which Peter is up on a housetop praying. He has a marvelous vision, and then very matter-of-factly the New Testament records that ''the Spirit said unto him, behold three men seek thee. Arise, . . . and get thee down, and go with them . . . for I have sent them.'' (Acts 10:19.) It sounds as natural as a telephone call, doesn't it? Peter knew what to do; he knew three men were coming for him. He knew he should get down from the housetop and join them. The Lord gave him direction.

Likewise the Book of Mormon tells how God's servants were tuned to the Spirit. Nephi records: ''And I was led by the Spirit, not knowing beforehand the things which I should do'' (1 Nephi 4:6). The prophet Alma contended with Zeezrom and taught him that "God . . . knows all thy thoughts, and thou seest that thy thoughts are made known unto us by his Spirit" (Alma 12:3).

Now, if we are to make of this life what we would, we must be guided by the Lord. A trial-and-error existence will never get us where we want to be. We must ask for his help, expect it, and then act upon it when it comes. And we can do that if we have developed our special spiritual ears and sensitivities to pick up the messages the Lord is sending us. The migrating birds couldn't reach their goal without their special physical senses, and frankly, we will never reach our goals without our special spiritual ones. How sad for the Lord to send us a message only to find our receiver out of order!

A young officer in the air force in World War II was assigned to train other young men how to fly. This officer was a man who had learned to hear the Lord and rely on him for guidance. One day before he was to go up on a particular flight, he prayed as he always did that the Lord would protect him. Later, when he and his student pilot were up flying, he suddenly felt fear, real and tangible, clutch his body. The hairs on his neck were standing on end. Why, he thought, did he feel this way? The sky was blue and clear. Not another plane was in sight, but the fear was the worst he had ever known. He seemed to hear a voice telling him to take the controls away from the student pilot, so in an instance he grabbed them and said, "I've got it." Following the spiritual message he was hearing, he turned the flight stick abruptly right and the plane veered sharply off its course. At that very second another plane coming up on an angle from below crossed the path they would have been on. It was impossible to see the plane; they had no way of knowing it was there. But if the officer hadn't listened to the message and turned his plane, they would have collided, inevitably and fatally. The officer had prayed for protection and the Lord had answered that prayer, but most important of all, the officer had learned what answers sound and feel like.

I'm impressed that migrating birds pick up so much real and actual stimuli from the environment that we cannot. And I am more impressed that some people are so much more adept at picking up spiritual stimuli, having trained their senses and hearts to know what they are. The Lord has counseled, ''Be still and know that I am God.'' We all need direction from the Lord in our lives. And as we ask him for it, he is continuing to send it to us. Let us listen and not tune him out.

19

The Best Invention

When you consider all of the modern conveniences there are in the world today, which would you feel are the most necessary? I remember reading an article by one of the world's experts on the greatest inventions of all time. I suppose that no two people would ever agree on any selection made by experts, but I found the list most stimulating. See what you think:

1. The alphabet. While there is no question as to the value of early Egyptian hieroglyphics, their function was limited. Imagine trying to write a nuclear equation that way (or your shopping list).

2. The wheel. Probably one of the greatest invention of all time. Almost all advances have come as a result of the wheel.

3. The inner flange of the wheel. This invention has made the railroads what they are. Think of the impact the railroad has had on history.

4. The electric battery. This invention makes possible 80 percent of all industry today.

5. The radio. Daily communication has brought the world into our home and daily lives. (Watch teenagers today.)

6. Glass. Try existing without windows in your house, car, office, etc.

7. The match has revolutionized the world more than almost any single item.

8. Paper. The countries of the world would find it difficult to exist without it. (Some organizations might do better.)

9. The loom. Clothing has played a dominant role in all societies. (Ask my family.)

10. Fabricating of metal into tools. Think of our dependency upon tools and metals.

Well, there they are. You and I would probably delete some and add others. While all ten inventions have had a profound effect on the human race, there are others that I believe are even more effective though not as tangible. Perhaps the greatest of all inventions is the one stated by Mirabeau when he said: "If honesty did not exist, we ought to invent it as the best means of getting rich."

Let me modify that statement and make it even more valid. "If honesty did not exist, we ought to invent it as the best means of discovering true wealth."

Benjamin Franklin said it best: "Honesty is the best policy." That is not only a great statement, it is an eternal principle. An honest dating policy is best; an honest communication policy is best; an honest marriage policy is best; an honest financial policy is best; an honest foreign policy is best. George Washington made a statement about such policies which has become a classic. It bears repeating: "I hope that I shall always possess firmness and virtue enough to maintain what I consider the most enviable of all titles, the character of an honest man.''

Think about that statement for a moment. While honesty may be more often discovered than invented, it is a principle each must find for himself. We can hear it taught or read about it, but until we experience it for ourselves, it isn't ours. One of the sad commentaries is to observe those who struggled in life situations to discover the value of honesty. Some years ago a colleague of mine shared this experience which was later printed.

"I had stressed the need for honesty, explaining to my students that many times we don't even know our integrity is being tested. I had shared with them experiences like Mr. Larkin's at the corner drugstore. He had told me that Alfred could not be trusted.

" 'How do you know?' I inquired.

" 'Well,' he said, 'often when I have lots of customers and I'm the only salesperson in the store, I let young people make their own change from the cash drawer. I started coming up short, so I carefully counted out the cash before and after several youngsters had made their own change. They were all honest with me except Alfred. I gave him two chances, and he failed me both times. So now I know that Alfred can't be trusted.'

" 'Have you told him?' I asked.

" 'No, I never have. I just watch him very closely. I hope he never asks me for a job or for a recommendation.'

"So my class should have been prepared for the snap quiz I gave them that Thursday afternoon. It was a twenty-question, true-or-false test covering material we had discussed during the week. They finished the test just as the bell rang for dismissal.

" 'Please pass your papers to the center of the aisle,' I instructed.

"Later that evening I very carefully graded each paper, recording the score in my grade book but leaving no marks on the papers.

"When the class assembled the next morning, I passed the papers back and, as usual, asked that each student grade his own paper.

"I read each question aloud and with a word of explanation announced the correct answer. Every answer was accompanied by the usual student groan or sigh of relief at having given a wrong or right response.

" 'Please count five off for each one missed and subtract the total from one hundred,' I instructed. 'Your scores please.

" 'John?'

" '85.'

" 'Susan?'

" '95.'

" 'Harold?'

" '80.'

" 'Arnold?'

" '90.'

" 'Mary?'

"The response could hardly be heard: '45.'

"I went on, putting the grades in my grade book, carefully recording each oral report next to the grade I had recorded the night before. The comparison was revealing.

"A stillness settled on the class when I explained what I had done. Many did not look up from their desks; others exchanged furtive glances or quick smiles.

"I spoke quietly to my students.

" 'Some of you may wish to talk to me privately about our experience here today. I would like that.

" 'This was a different kind of test. This test was a test for honesty. Were you true or false? I noticed that many of you looked at Mary when she announced her score of 45. Mary, if you don't mind, would you please stand up? I want each of you to know that in my book Mary just achieved the highest score in the class. You make me feel very proud, Mary.'

"Mary looked up rather timidly at first, then her eyes glistened as she broke into a smile and rose to her feet. I had never seen Mary stand so tall." (Wayne B. Lynn, "True . . . or . . . False," *New Era,* September 1978, p. 11.)

Alexander Pope described people like Mary in this way: "An honest person is the noblest work of God." It is obvious that in the above class situation, several students tried to tamper with honesty. But many, I am sure, learned a great lesson that changed lives.

Occasionally I have smiled at true life situations where individuals attempting to be honest found it difficult to convey their experience. An insurance company has shared some classic statements they discovered on insurance accident report forms. A client wrote: "I was on my way to the doctor with rear end trouble when my universal joint gave way, causing me to have an accident."

Here's another: "The pedestrian had no idea which direction to run, so I ran over him."

Another: "I saw a slow-moving sad-faced old gentleman as he bounced off the hood of my car."

And then: "I pulled away from the side of the road, glanced at my mother-in-law, and headed over the embankment."

We may smile, but who hasn't found it difficult to be totally honest. An unknown author has said: "There are four types of honesty: (1) That which exists as long as it pays. (2) That which exists for fear of punitive consequences. (3) That which exists for fear of criticism. (4) The genuine, born of true moral fiber.''

In the spirit of genuine honesty, some years ago the Church distributed posters and cards which challenged all to ''Be Honest with Yourself.'' It is a theme most would agree is basic and practical. There is no question but what the principle of honesty would greatly improve society and enhance our own spiritual dimension and personality. To abstain from robbing or cheating is certainly in harmony with God's commandments, but what about being totally honest with oneself? What about questions such as: Do I have personal habits that might offend others? Are my weight and personal appearance what they ought to be in order to be more acceptable to friends and associates? Is my attitude one of wanting to help or assist others or am I more concerned about me? Am I able to accept counsel and constructive criticism from others? What about my personal growth in educational and spiritual pursuits? All too often problems in these areas can result in our being alone or not accepted. When we are not honest with ourselves, it is easy to blame other sources or situations. Clouds of despair, feeling left out in the rain, and never finding the rainbow seem to result in periods of depression.

Joshua Liebman, author of *Peace of Mind*, points out that it is normal for everyone to have periods of depression. Job was so depressed that he longed for death, and Jeremiah apparently was so dejected that he cursed the day he was born. Perhaps as we honestly ask questions about ourselves we may well fall victim to depression or discouragement. But if we are to solve our dilemmas we must do as Benjamin Franklin suggests:

''Let honesty be as the breath of thy soul; then shalt thou reach the point of happiness, and independence shall be thy shield and buckler, thy helmet and crown; then shall thy soul walk upright, nor stoop to the silken wretch because he hath riches, nor pocket an abuse because the hand which offers it wears a ring set with diamonds.''

Let us remember that one who desires a reputation for honesty must first pay the price, which is eternal vigilance and diligence. Honesty, like gold, is very much in demand. It is precious because there is no adequate substitute for it, and because it is so rare. May each of us invent honesty in our own lives and discover true wealth.

IV

The Passing
of the Storm

20

On Making Mistakes

Life is full of funny mistakes. When Senator Mike Mansfield was first elected to the Senate after serving five terms in the House of Representatives, he and his wife, Maureen, decided to buy a new house in the Washington, D.C., area. She shopped around for a house and finally found one she liked very much but couldn't get her husband to take even an hour away from his busy schedule to come and see it. She pleaded and pleaded and on the day the final decision was to be made, Mansfield agreed he'd meet her at the house, but he never showed up. So she went ahead and bought the house without his seeing it. When she approached him later to find out why he had never come to the house as he had promised, she found out the funny news. He had been waiting for an hour in front of the House of Representatives. (''Personal Glimpses,'' *Reader's Digest*, April 1976, p. 126.)

Well, we all make mistakes. Sometimes they are big bloopers, other times just little errors, but nobody is immune to them. As much as we hate to admit it, to be human is to err. In fact, it is so common to be wrong even about the basic facts we think we know that Tom Burnam put together a dictionary of misinformation. Here are some of the tidbits found there. Did you know, for example, that the Battle of Bunker Hill was not really fought on Bunker Hill at all? It was fought on Breed's Hill nearby. The original report of the battle contained the error and it was never corrected. Did you know that Mrs. O'Leary's famous cow that supposedly started the Chicago fire really had nothing to do with it? The cow couldn't have kicked over a lantern while being milked, for it had been milked much earlier and Mrs. O'Leary was resting peacefully in bed when the fire broke out. And did you know that at no point in Arthur Conan Doyle's fifty-six short stories did Sherlock Holmes ever utter the famous words, "Elementary, my dear Watson." (Tom Burnam, *The Dictionary of Misinformation* [New York: Thomas Y. Crowell Company, 1975], pp. 33, 161, 227.)

Well, unfortunately we don't know everything, and we simply don't do everything right. But you can tell the person who really wants to progress in this world because he is the one who dares show himself as vulnerable. He is not afraid to learn something new, even if it exposes his ignorance. He doesn't always have to appear to be right, because he knows that the acquisition of any new skill or knowledge necessarily involves the admission that he doesn't know all things yet. He can't be all things perfectly —at least not yet.

In fact, the very secret of self-confidence is being able to make a mistake and not be devastated by it.

Those who achieve most in this world are those who are willing to put themselves on the line, who move from the safe but confining stance of invulnerability to try something new.

Think about it. An eight-year-old child wants to learn to play the piano, but she hates being corrected. It's painful. She wants to do it perfectly the first time and get all the applause that goes with it. But even playing "Clare de Lune" demands practice, making an error and then trying to correct it, and then maybe even making that error again, all of which are part of the learning process. If you have ever learned to play a musical instrument, you know that there are plenty of painful hours listening to yourself. If you give up at that point because you hate to be less than perfect, you never arrive at Chopin.

The same is true in science. For every great discovery, for every scientific breakthrough, a scientist has seen many of his pet theories proven wrong. He has seen trial and error and repeated failure, but has nevertheless progressed because of it, for with every idea that was proven wrong in the cold world of fact, he at least knew one more thing that didn't work. Edison tried at least one thousand substances for the filament for the light bulb before he found something that worked. And Madame Curie sifted through a lot of coal before she found radium. This meant, of course, that many nights Edison and Curie went to bed feeling like failures, knowing that during that day they had made errors and miscalculations, but they obviously had enough self-confidence to live with it and keep trying.

And in literature it is the same. How many aspiring writers have filled wastepaper baskets with crumpled paper, the cans filled with snatches of thought that didn't develop, words that were inadequate to meet the idea. One popular writer says she routinely goes through her manuscripts before they are printed and cuts out at least a tenth of them, ruthlessly red penciling sentences and paragraphs to make the story tighter.

And yet, we look at people's accomplishments in music, science, or literature, or in any field of endeavor, and we think, "Wouldn't it be nice to be so expert? Wouldn't it be wonderful to excel with so little difficulty, to be beyond mistakes?" But we must not fool ourselves. Getting there involves lots of awkward hours and self-questioning. The best among us are those who dare to make mistakes and dare to stick it out to correct them. Those of us who would rather appear above error remain mediocre.

The famous heart surgeon Michael Debakey tells this story about his surgical training under Dr. Alton Ochsner. It seems that "Ochsner had opened a patient's rib cage one day in 1938 at the Charity Hospital of Louisiana in New Orleans. Trainee Debakey, assisting him before an assembly of surgeons, pulled back the aorta, precisely, he hoped, as Ochsner had instructed him to do. Whether because of his nervousness or the patient's weakened tissue, his index finger, exerting a milligram too much pressure, punctured the patient's aorta, the major artery leading from the heart. Fearing he had just killed the patient, he whispered the news to Ochsner, who, to his astonishment, said calmly, 'Just leave your finger there. Don't pull it out.' Deftly, Ochsner sutured around the wound in the aorta wall, then said, 'Gingerly now, pull your finger out.'

" 'Ochsner could, at that moment, have destroyed my confidence—and my career,' Debakey concludes. 'But he did not. He did not curse me, nor embarrass me. He treated it as a simple mistake.' "

("Personal Glimpses," *Reader's Digest*, February 1977, p. 29.)

If we are going to progress in this life, we must be willing to make mistakes, to tread into territory where we are not expert. The fronts we put up in order to appear wonderfully competent to our fellows may be fine for a while, but there will always be the nagging feelings inside that tell us we could be something more. On our first leap for the stars, we may only hit the top of the tree and feel silly dangling there before our friends, but leap we must. The Lord would have us leap, and reach, and try, daring to expose ourselves as imperfect on the way to becoming perfect. That you and I may have the confidence to try is my hope for us all.

21

Wearing Yourself Out

The other day, after many long hours in my assignment, I arrived home rather late and said to my wife, "I'm worn out." And I suppose I had a right to be physically exhausted after what I had been through that day, but I've noticed that in today's demanding world these words, "I'm worn out," are repeated all too often. I have also noticed that children do *not* use the phrase. Instead of making that comment they simply go to sleep when they can't hold their eyes open any longer.

I suppose age itself can eventually take its toll on the body, as can boredom and everyday routine, sometimes as much if not more than physical effort. We have all had the experience of being "tired" on days when there was no physical exertion at all, and I have finally come to the conclusion that wearing out is often really a state of mind. And as far as age is concerned, reduced activity doesn't mean that minds must wear out. In fact, we all know people well into their eighties and beyond who, *because* of active minds and positive attitudes, have remarkable energy levels. For example, take the attitude of Jimmy Durante, the great comedian of our time who performed vigorously until the day he died. Here's an example of his mind-set and philosophy.

"It happened shortly after World War II. One day he received a call from Ed Sullivan. Sullivan wanted Durante to accompany him to a veterans' hospital to entertain the many wounded and disabled vets there.

"Durante told [Mr. Sullivan] he'd like to go, but he had two very remunerative radio shows to do on [the date in question]. Sullivan assured him they could drive out early and get back in time for Durante's engagements. Durante agreed but told Sullivan that he would only have time for one number.

"The two drove out the following Sunday and Durante did his number. The audience was ecstatic and pleaded for more. What happened then surprised even Sullivan, who was well aware that Durante must leave immediately for the city if he was to meet his radio dates. Durante accepted the applause, then proceeded to do two more routines!

"When he finally made his exit to a standing ovation from the vets, Sullivan cried, 'Jimmy, you were just great. But now you'll never make your radio shows.'

" 'Look at the front row of the audience,' Durante told him. 'You'll see why I forgot all about those dates.'

"Sullivan poked his head through the curtain and spotted two soldiers in the center of the front row. Each had lost an arm, and they were applauding by clapping their two remaining hands together."

I suppose as a performer Jimmy often wore himself out. But his feelings and resulting acts of compassion, like the one just mentioned, kept him going and made him the unforgettable character he was. Kindness and compassion have strength that the physical side has not known. The Talmud puts it this way: There are ten strong things. Iron is strong, but fire melts it. Fire is strong, but water quenches it. Water is strong, but the sun evaporates it. The sun is strong, but clouds can cover it. Clouds are strong, but wind can drive clouds away. Wind is strong, but man can shut it out. Man is strong, but fears cast him down. Fear is strong, but sleep overcomes it. Sleep is strong, yet death is stronger. But the strongest is kindness. It survives death.

While time will wear us all out eventually, so will doing deeds of kindness and compassion. And if we're going to tire either way, why not do so in the service of others? The results of that kind of time spent will live on forever and will bless our lives as we have blessed the lives of those around us. I do not believe we have to be a Jimmy Durante to lift others. Our service can be given in small ways and can be done quietly. I have to smile even as I say that because of a little anecdote I once read:

"A cluster of small boys, obviously without the price of admission, milled about near one of the entrance gates to a football stadium. An observer said to the ticket-taker in a voice resonant with authority. 'Let these kids in and tell me how many there are.' The boys filed in and scampered delightedly into the crowd. As the last one entered the ticket-taker said to the observer, 'Thirty-four,' The man nodded. 'Right you are,' he said, as he disappeared in the crowd outside the gate." (*Soundings*, April 1988, p. 9.) While we might well question the man's method, his motive was great!

I love the Savior for many reasons, but in particular I love him for his sensitive and compassionate nature. I love to read the scriptural account of his life and of his appearance to those on both continents. His words of kindness make me rejoice. Note: ''Rise, take up thy bed and walk''; ''Go, and sin no more''; ''Damsel, I say unto thee, arise''; ''Lazarus, come forth.'' The list goes on and on.

The hard part for most of us is another phrase used by the Savior. It's a simple one, but vital to our becoming ''worn out.'' Jesus said, ''Go, and do thou likewise'' (Luke 10:37).

I really believe that the Lord meant us to do that and that we ought to give it a try, even though it's not always easy or convenient.

Allow me to make a suggestion. If you really want to feel the happiness of wearing yourself out in a good cause, why don't you just drive over to one of our local old folks homes some evening and go on in. Ask to be permitted to visit with one of the ''less visited.'' Then just sit down and talk to this great person. Or read her a story, or just sit and listen. Perhaps you will want to hold her hand, or even help with a meal. Chances are she won't know you or, perhaps, even herself. But spend a half hour or so with her. Really give of yourself. Then, when you're through, go home and eat dinner. I'll wager that your meal will never have tasted better. You'll be emotionally exhausted. And you'll feel better than you have in years. Give it a try.

I believe the advice I am giving both you and me is sound. The Spirit will testify to that. But like many things, talking and doing are two different issues. I can remember as a young man lying in bed and dreaming of becoming a great baseball pitcher. But when the alarm went off it was time to stop dreaming and start doing. It was a great major league pitcher himself, Johnny Sain, who compressed this idea into two sentences. It's a classic: "The world doesn't want to hear about the labor pains. It only wants to see the baby." Not bad for an athlete.

An anonymous writer has said:

> Somebody did a golden deed;
> Somebody proved a friend in need;
> Somebody sang a beautiful song;
> Somebody smiled the whole day long;
> Somebody thought, "Tis sweet to live";
> Somebody said, "I'm glad to give";
> Somebody fought a valiant fight;
> Somebody lived to shield the right;
> Was that "Somebody" you?

May I encourage us all to take this great idea of caring and really do something with it in our lives. The results will surprise us. I am reminded of the story of a man who gave a woman his seat on the bus. She fainted. When she came to, she thanked him. He fainted.

Well, let's not cause people to faint with surprise, but if we implement this feeling of compassion and kindness into our lives, husbands will surely surprise wives, children will surprise parents, and neighbors will surprise neighbors. What could be more exciting for all!

One more time: since we are all going to wear ourselves out in this life anyway, one way or another, may we do so in either small or great but *consistent* acts of kindness.

If we do, I am confident that the following lines from Tennyson will be fulfilled in our behalf:

Crossing the Bar

> Sunset and evening star,
>   And one clear call for me!

And may there by no moaning of the bar,
   When I put out to sea,

. . . .

Twilight and evening bell,
   And after that the dark!
And may there be no sadness of farewell,
   When I embark;
For tho' from out our bourne of Time and Place
   The flood may bear me far,
I hope to see my Pilot face to face
   When I have crost the bar.

   May we all be so blessed then for wearing ourselves out for him *now!*

22

Your Last Will
and Testament

Several years ago I was touched by a local newspaper article telling of an unfortunate experience which occurred in Chicago. The account stated:

"The policeman walked the length of the freight train, the red nose sniffing, a mittened hand holding a night stick. Chicago was cold. The cop's stick pulled along the rows of icicles hanging from a refrigerator car like a boy with a board running the length of a picket fence. The icicles fell.

"He came to a car with open doors and he rapped the stick hard. No hobos inside. The policeman hoisted himself up in the door. The car was empty. No, there was a pile of old rags in a dark corner. He climbed up. His feet were so cold they tingled with warmth.

"He prodded the bundle of rags with the stick. There was something hard inside. He looked. Then he hurried out of the car and up the right of way to a telephone. 'A frozen bum,' he said. 'Send the meat wagon.' The cop looked at his watch. Three forty-five. He was off at four. This thing would require overtime. An autopsy. Darn those bums!

"The unknown, unmissed man was crouched with his knees up, his frozen fingers clasped around his legs. The ambulance driver sat him on a stretcher. The railroad policeman appreciated the warmth of the bus. He blew on his hands and looked at the face of the man for the first time. Old. Wispy hair, still alive, moving up and down the scalp. Saffron skin. Unshaved whiskers. Half-opened eyes. Bony hands with dirty fingernails.

"The morgue was warm with green tile. An attendant cut off the rags. The old man looked older. No identification. Inside the dirty shirt was a wrinkled sheet of paper. It was tossed to the cop. He read it as the pathologist worked on what was left of a human being.

" 'This,' the paper said in shaky handwriting, 'is my last will and testament. No one knows me, no one will miss me, and I have nothing of substance to leave anyone. Sentiment impels me to leave something to all the lovely people in a lovely world. So—

" 'To all the elderly, I leave only the fond and bright memories of other days; reminiscenses of babies plump and tender; of nights when love was warm and fresh; of rewarding works and supple hands and minds; of love coming now from new babies which, while they may belong to others, give richly of their wet kisses and gummy smiles . . .

" 'To children, I leave the green summery fields to run in; the dark, cool streams to swirl around bare feet; the buttery sun to stay high forever; the crack of bat on baseball; jacks for playing on the hot sidewalk; ropes for double-Dutch jumping; birthday parties and gifts every week; and most of all—innocence . . .

" 'To young lovers, I bequeath the full silvery moon; endless dreams of two becoming one; the uncounted riches of true romance; the twining of warm hands; hope chest; rings; an ecstatic feel over the horizon at all the happy tomorrows; but, most of all, I leave you each other . . .

" 'To the poor, my legacy is hope; I cut you off from despair; disillusionment, and resignation; I wish for you good food, a roof of your own, a future growing brighter each day, a determination to rise above the harshness of chill winds and heartless strangers; I leave to you forgiveness of self and the riches of others . . .

" 'To the rich, I leave another God, one laden with mercy and understanding; I bequeath to you also a mint of charity and pity for others; a treasury of poor boxes, and compassion for those whose lives you control; above all, I bequeath to you the humbling knowledge that some day all the shiny coins will cascade in a waterfall from between your fingers . . .

" 'To the infants, I leave the center of the universe; the love of your parents; a soft breast; dreams of angels; the joy of seeing Daddy come through the front door in the evening; a rubber ring to chew on; above all, the same future I have already left for lovers . . .'

"The cop folded the paper. There was no signature. He looked at his watch. He turned away from the pathologist and his work. 'Find out anything?' he said. The doctor grunted. 'Preliminary finding is malnutrition. I don't know how long he was in that freight car, but he starved and froze to death. Anything on that piece of paper?'

" 'Nothing,' the policeman said, 'just the raving of a nut.' He had the sniffles again. The doctor wagged his head. 'Strange,' he said, 'this man must have thought that piece of paper was important, he kept it next to his heart.' "

This experience brought to my mind another unusual will that was originally filed in the probate court of Cook County, Illinois, by another unknown author. It read:

"I, being of sound and disposing mind and memory, do hereby make and publish this, my last will and testament, in order as to justly as may be, to distribute my interest in the world among succeeding men.

"That part of my interest which is known in law and recognized in the sheep-bound volumes as my property, being inconsiderable and of no account, I make no disposition of this in my will. My right to live, being but a life estate, is not at my disposal, but, these things excepted, all else in the world I now proceed to devise and bequeath.

"Item: I give to good fathers and mothers, in trust for their children, all good little words of praise and encouragement, and all quaint pet names and endearment; and I charge said parents to use them justly, but generously, as the deeds of their children shall require.

"Item: I leave to children inclusively, but only for the term of their childhood, all and every flower of the field and the blossoms of the woods, with the right to play among them freely according to the custom of children, warning them at the same time against thistles and thorns. And I devise to children the banks of the brooks and the golden sands beneath the waters thereof, and the odors of the willows that dip therein, and the white clouds that float high over giant trees. And I leave the children the long, long days to be merry in, in a thousand ways, and the night and the train of the Milky Way to wonder at, but subject, nevertheless to the rights hereinafter given to lovers.

"Item: I devise to boys, jointly, all the useful idle fields and commons where ball may be played, all pleasant waters where one may swim, all snowclad hills where one may coast, and all streams and ponds where one may fish, or where, when grim winter comes, one may skate, to hold the same period of their boyhood. And all meadows with the clover-blossoms and butterflies thereof; the woods with their beauty; the squirrels and the birds and the echoes and their strange noises, and all distant places, which may be visited, together with the adventures there found. And I give to said boys each his own place at the fireside at night, with all pictures that may be seen in the burning wood, to enjoy without let or kindrance or without any encumbrance or care.

"Item: To lovers, I devise their imaginary world, with whatever they may need, as the stars of the sky, the red roses by the wall, the bloom of the hawthorn, the sweet strains of music, and aught else they may desire to figure to each other the lastingness and beauty of their love.

"Item: To young men jointly, I bequeath all the boisterous, inspiring sports of rivalry, and I give to them the disdain of weakness and undaunted confidence in their own strength. Though they are rude, I leave to them the power to make lasting friendships, and of possessing companions, and to them, exclusively, I give all merry songs and grave choruses to sing with lusty voices.

"Item: And to those who are no longer children or youths or lovers, I leave memory; and bequeath to them volumes of poems of Burns and Shakespeare and of other poets, if there be others, to the end that they may live in the old days again, freely and fully without tithe or diminution.

"Item: To our loved ones with snowy crowns, I bequeath the happiness of old age, the love and gratitude of their children until they fall asleep."

Certainly these last wills and testaments show great insight and feeling. In today's world much emphasis has been given to making wills and family trusts. To be prepared for the inevitable is wise planning, and we need not place our loved ones in untenable situations.

Too often families are left to argue or squabble over a loved one's estate rather than finding fulfillment in carrying out that loved one's wishes and desires. Frequently greed and selfishness become the criteria for settling a dispute.

Perhaps you are familiar with the fable involving a group of people who lived in a provincial section of a jungle:

Once upon a time in the days before anything much was organized and when people were all pretty much alike and had not learned to be doctors and bookmakers and husbands or milkmen, there were never any holidays because everyone was too busy.

What they were busy doing was . . . *taking stuff.*

They spent all of their time either taking stuff, or trying to take stuff, or planning to take stuff from each other, or fixing the walls and fences and barbwire in their section of the jungle so no one could take stuff from them.

In those days it was considered most necessary to have a lot of stuff, and taking it gave people a stimulating feeling. When they took something especially good (i.e., big), the feeling started in the back of their backs and spread down across their back and made a tingle in their left foot. This feeling was the only feeling anyone ever had except maybe being scared or being hungry.

Several techniques were used: first, swiping. This was the most difficult because naturally few people were foolish enough to leave any of their stuff unguarded.

The second and most popular method was to find someone smaller than you and give him an unexpected bash. Then you could grab his stuff and run. This method, although dangerous, had the advantage of being healthful, as the bashing and running promoted deep breathing and kept the waistline down.

Now, in time, the smaller people learned to be very clever, hiding and swiping, and the large developed a protective layer of bone across the back of their skulls, and some of the medium-sized discovered that they could tell big lies about the amount of stuff they had hidden and this was about the same as actually having the stuff.

And so a status quo came to exist. It balanced out pretty well for everyone, that is, everyone except Marvin Ouk.

Marvin Ouk lived in a rather provincial section of the jungle, and his only neighbors were named Gloog, Howk, Murdleigh, and Lester.

Now Gloog, Howk, Murdleigh, and Lester had each accumulated exactly the same amount of stuff. They were all of about the same size, and they had equally excellent walls, and so it became difficult for them to increase their stuff. One day Murdleigh would bash Gloog and take his shirt and eggbeater, but the next day Howk would bash Murdleigh and take his shirt and fountain pen, and so on.

They were all getting bashed a great deal, and in the long run there was no percentage in it. So after a while they all concentrated mostly on taking stuff from Marvin, which wasn't easy.

Marvin was the smallest, the most simple-minded, and the least devious of all the people. He didn't even have a proper wall or fence, and as a result he had no stuff. In fact, Marvin never had anything. He didn't even have a pair of pants (which slowed him down socially). He lived on a diet of toadstools (these being the only things he could depend on not being taken), and the only feeling he ever experienced was not getting hit, which he considered enjoyable.

So it wasn't long before Gloog and Howk and Murdleigh and Lester even gave up trying to take stuff from Marvin. It wasn't worth the trouble it took to bash him because, although he bashed easily, Marvin was concussion prone and merely fell quietly face forward and didn't yell or holler or do anything fun.

And so in this part of the jungle the status "-quoed" more than was suitable. Actually the status became "over-quoed," and Gloog and Howk and Murdleigh and Lester sat behind their walls and got restless.

"It is not right to not take stuff," Murdleigh said. "One should get more stuff. It is the way things are." He would then go out and try to sneak up on Gloog or catch Howk or swipe something from Lester. But he never could.

Then he would go back home and fret some more. "I will forget how to take stuff," he would tell himself. "I will lose my technique." And one day he added, "I must keep in practice or my know-how will desert me."

So he rushed out and found Marvin Ouk and in his mind he pretended that Marvin was carrying a double armful of stuff. He then gave Marvin an excellent bash and pretended to take the imaginary stuff away from him, but it didn't work. He didn't get any feeling or tingle at all.

He went back home and fretted some more. "It was not playing the game to pretend," he told himself, and he began to think. After a bit he had an idea. "Umm," he said, "if I'm going to practice on Marvin, I must play the game. He must have something to take, so I will go out and . . . he paused and made up a word to express the odd idea he had in mind. "Give," he said, "I will give Marvin something first. Then I can take it."

When Marvin saw him he sighed and looked about for a soft spot to fall forward on. He was, of course, surprised, even shocked, when Murdleigh stopped in front of him and made no bashing gestures. "Ouk," said Murdleigh, making a peculiar and frightening grimace (which men later learned to call a "smile"), "Ouk, I have some stuff here I want to give you." He pushed a spoon toward Marvin. Marvin backed away. "Murdleigh has sprung a gasket," he thought. "I shall carefully go away as he may become dangerous."

But Murdleigh anticipated Marvin's escape and seized him by the arm. "Here," he said, and placed the spoon in Marvin's hand, "I want you to *have* this."

Then he stepped back and prepared to give Marvin a bash and take the stuff in the approved manner, but before he could move, he felt a strange new feeling! A feeling ten times more powerful than the feeling he had when he took stuff. It started in the back of his chest and spread, not only through his back and his left foot, but all over. He began to tingle in both feet and both hands and on top of his head. The new feeling was so pleasant and so powerful that Murdleigh caught his breath and sat down on the ground.

"Ha," he said, and again made the terrible grimace in Marvin's direction. Marvin turned and raced away.

"Who would have suspected?" said Murdleigh. "Giving stuff is . . ." He searched for a "noise" he could use, another new word. "Ooser?" he said, and then "Meepy?" Then he tried "Misser," and then "Nicer."

"Nicer" sounded exactly right. "Giving stuff," Murdleigh said, "is nicer than taking stuff."

Murdleigh soon found out that part of the new feeling was a desire to tell other people about it, and he did; and so another great discovery was made.

What a great discovery! Giving stuff is nicer than taking stuff. Perhaps one of the great lessons we can learn from such experiences is to give while we can. Have you ever given serious thought as to what you would really like to give to your posterity? Much of our true value and worth we can give while we are yet alive—joy, comfort, good times, memories, and a host of others.

Henry Van Dyke said: "Some people are so afraid to die that they never begin to live. And some people are so afraid to live . . . that they wait until it's too late to start."

May we both start and live and give now to those we love and cherish.

23

Time Waits for No One

Several years ago I had a college friend whose chief interest was studying, so he gathered all the needed equipment. He procured a large comfortable chair that was thought to be good for study. He provided slippers and comfortable clothes, and a bookrest was fastened to the arm of the chair to hold the book at the right angle before his eyes. A special lamp with proper shades was installed to cast the light just right. He would come home in the evening, take off his coat and shoes, slip into his jeans and slippers, adjust the study lamp, put his book on the bookrest, recline in the comfortable chair, and when everything was perfectly adjusted, he would go to sleep.

Ever wonder where your life goes? Have you ever heard people say: "Life sure passed me by," or "I can't believe how time flies," or "I just can't find time," or "There are not enough hours in the day."

Sound familiar? It seems to me all of us have said something like that at one time or another. In fact, in our fast-moving world those statements are made more and more often. Statisticians tell us that if we live to be seventy and lead an "average life" we'll spend:

13 years gaining an education
8 years at the dinner table
5 years in traveling
4 years in conversation (perhaps
   a little longer for some)
14 years in work
3 years in reading
24 years in sleeping

That seems pretty cut and dried. But I wonder. Anyway, here's a good question: How is it that some of our fellow travelers not only find time to dream but also to make their dreams come true?

Perhaps many who are discouraged or have lost hope should ask themselves how their time has been invested. Of course, there are myriad reasons why we don't make our dreams come true—and an equal number of solutions to the problem. But after all is said and done, a great part of the reason we don't is because we don't plan and use our time wisely. Somehow we aren't always willing to pay the price in time.

Let's take an example: Remember the average life of seventy years? Suppose a young man seeks a close and personal relationship with his Father in Heaven: that's his dream! Well, if he goes to church every week and prays five minutes each morning and night, he will be giving fifteen months to God. Fifteen months out of a life of seventy years. Is that enough? Will his dream be realized by spending fifteen months' worth of his time? Isn't there more to it than that?

How about a father and mother whose dream and goal in life is to be good parents, to be close to their children. Is that a realistic dream? I believe it is. What it takes is good common sense and time. Children love parents who, from the beginning, are willing to spend time with them. A nighttime story takes five minutes. Helping with homework may take half an hour (except for new math). Sincerely listening to a teenager's concern or problem may take a little time each day. An outing together may take two hours. Working in the yard together may take a half a day a week. Going on vacation together may take two weeks a year. But it all adds up. And where time is ungrudgingly given, dreams come true.

Even though "time flies on wings of lightning," we can certainly determine the direction it takes. If you use it well, it will be your friend. If you try to kill it, it will most surely be your enemy.

Ellis Shipp is a little-known but fascinating pioneer woman. She was married at the age of nineteen to Milford Shipp. Nine days after her third son was born, her husband was called on a two-year mission to Europe. Ellis supported her little family with no more than a cow, an orchard, and a garden plot. She sewed and knitted and took in a student boarder, but was not satisfied with her ability to care for and educate her children. She had had only one year of formal schooling and so she developed a plan of study, arising every morning at 4:00 A.M. so she could daily put in three solid hours of study before her husband returned from his mission. Various entries in her diary relate her early morning program of studying poetry, history, English grammar, hygiene, and health. She became Utah's second woman doctor.

Imagine getting up every morning at 4:00 A.M. Time can really make a difference, and the great thing about it is that we generally have as much of it as anybody else. It's up to us how we use it.

I have a good friend who is a doctor. He's a heart specialist and one of the best in the world. He has paid the price to become that kind of doctor. But do you know the best thing about my friend? He still has taken time to become a great husband and father. He also uses his time to be involved in many other activities. And he somehow finds time to hold a responsible position in his church.

I know another young man who is using part of his time to accomplish his dream of becoming a great lawyer. His family doesn't even have to nag to get him to night school. And so the story goes . . . on and on as people use this priceless commodity of time to fulfill their dreams.

Perhaps the most sought-after dream of all is that of being happy. Sometimes we aren't sure how to reach that goal, but we know that's what we want. We have a loving Father in Heaven who also wants us to be happy. That great Book of Mormon prophet Lehi taught that "men are, that they might have joy" (2 Nephi 2:25). He cares what happens to us and does as much for us as we'll let him do. He wants us to be happy now and return to him so that we can be happy in his presence forever. But so much depends on how we use our time. There are a couple of simple things we can do to make sure we use our time wisely. We can make sure our "dreams" are worthy of our time and effort, and then we can get busy and spend the time necessary to fulfill them.

There was once a man who said, "I think I'm undecided, but I'm not sure." That is an attitude to avoid!

The Lord will bless us as we strive to use the precious gift of time in doing things that will bring us and others happiness now and for eternity. Ponder the following:

Just for today I will try to live through this day only, and not try to tackle my whole life at once. I can do things for twelve hours that would overwhelm me if I thought I had to keep them up for a lifetime.

Just for today I will be happy. This assumes that what Abraham Lincoln said is true: "Most folks are about as happy as they make up their minds to be." Happiness is from within; it is not a matter of externals.

Just for today I will try to adjust myself to what is and not try to adjust everything to my own desires. I will take my family, my business, and my luck as they come and fit myself to them.

Just for today I will take care of my body. I will exercise it, care for it, nourish it, and not abuse it nor neglect it, so that it will be a perfect machine for my bidding.

Just for today I will try to strengthen my mind. I will learn something useful. I will not be a mental loafer. I will read something that requires effort, thought, and concentration.

Just for today I will exercise my soul in these ways: I will do somebody a good turn and not get found out. I will do at least two things I don't want to do, as William James suggests, just for exercise.

Just for today I will be agreeable. I will look as well as I can, dress as becomingly as possible, talk low, act courteously, be liberal with praise, criticize not at all, nor find fault with anything, and not try to regulate or improve anyone.

Just for today I will have a quiet period all by myself and relax. In this time segment I will think of God, so as to get a little more perspective to my life.

Remember, time is on our side if we use it wisely.

24

The Last Time

Today has an endless feel about it, doesn't it? You feel as if you will always be just this age, as if your children will always look just the way they do now. When it's summer, you feel as if you will always be sticky hot; and when it's cold, you wonder if you will ever see the sun again. Do you remember when you thought you'd always be in high school? Remember when you couldn't even think beyond being a child in your parent's home? The present is awfully demanding—it seems like the only permanent thing in the universe.

But we do have ways to mark off the time. Take, for example, the circle of the seasons, the holidays that find us once again pulling out last year's decorations and wondering that twelve months have passed, photo albums stuffed with pictures that make us laugh—Mom wearing skirts above her knees and Dad wearing baggy pants. Or how about a letter inviting us to a party that happened ten years ago. The only certain thing about the present is that before we can catch it, it will be the past. It flitters past us like a moth, dancing in the light for a second, then darting off into the night.

And maybe, too, it is because time is so fluid that we like to remember all the firsts in our lifetime. The first child born, with all the wonder at the continuing miracle of life. The first kiss. The first night spent in the new home. The first day you ever rode a two-wheeler. Your first time at anything announces itself as important. It says, "Remember me. I am full of promise."

But just as there are firsts in your life, there are lasts, too—plenty of them. You don't cherish them, and sometimes you don't even realize them for what they are, for your last time at anything doesn't announce itself as the last. But as surely as you breathe, there will be the last time your little boy will come and throw his arms around you to kiss you good night. Tomorrow he'll stride in as a grown man, too dignified for hugs. There'll be the last time your little girl will run through the house scattering dirt and dolls in every room. "This is the last time I'm going to tell you to stop it," you shout. And finally that last time really comes, for she becomes too big for dirt or dolls. She, who used to worry if she were separated from you by one aisle in a grocery store, will one day spend her last night sleeping in your house. She will have changed in some minute you didn't even know happened.

There'll be a last time the whole family will be together for Christmas. Those lovely traditions that seem so endless, being awakened a hundred times from four o'clock in the morning on, the making of sweet Christmas cookies—some day will be the last day for them.

And there will be the last time you look upon your parents' faces. The eyes that have always gazed on you so gently, the strong arms that have been a bulwark of security, the mouth that has smiled at you with understanding when the whole world called you worthless—there'll be a last time together. Oh, you may not know it. As I said, last times don't announce themselves, but even as you laugh together over a memory and chuckle with the mutual understanding that can only come for two who have known each other since first consciousness and first maturity, a final leaf is falling, a final page being written.

The last times. Life is full of them. The last time you felt the giddy frivolity of youth before responsibility set in. The last time you could fit into your wedding dress or suit. The last time you catch the hand of your mate, and give it an affectionate squeeze, a squeeze that says we can weather it—together. The last night in the home in which you've lived for twenty years. The next time you see it the new owners will have painted it or chopped down your favorite tree, and it will never be quite the same again. Yes, life has its lasts.

One woman said her nine-year-old boy had a respiratory infection. It didn't seem to be a serious one. But she helped him into bed one night, and as she turned off the light and was leaving the room, the boy said, "Mother, I love you. Please come and hold me." It was an unusual request from a boy so old, and though she had other tasks pressing her, she only hesitated a moment before she walked to his bedside. She held the little body close to her, and he looked up at her with sick eyes and a tired face. She had cherished that face for so long—when he, a baby, had first smiled, his eyes just focused enough to see her; when he, a chubby two-year-old, had made a stack of blocks ten high and then watched with giggles as it fell; when he had gone off to his first day of school and she had watched him growing smaller and smaller as he walked away; when he had the birthday that brought his baseball mitt. She had watched him through chicken pox, through the slice in his skin where a barbed wire fence had caught him. That slice had left the scar on what had been a perfect baby arm. And she had "kissed better" a thousand cuts and bruises, an ego shattered by the bumps of life. "Mother, I love you; please hold me." So she did, holding him until one arm had gone to sleep, until finally he had gone to sleep. And then through one of those awful twists that simple illness sometimes takes, he died during the night. She had held him for the last time. "The only comfort I have," she says regarding his death, "is that in his last conscious moment, he knew I loved him." Her memory of their last time together is a sweet one.

Now, I don't talk about last times to make you sad, but rather to help you realize that life is as transient as a season. Just as you have firsts, you have your lasts. And lasts are not to make you miserable, but to teach you that in a world where all things are fragile, you ought to properly appreciate them. You must handle with care your precious moments with loved ones. You must cherish your hours as unrepeatable. The number of moments for you on earth is finite. The endless stream of questions from your child really has an end, when he has grown to the point that he can satisfy his own curiosity. Even your face in the mirror will change.

So love what you love and love it hard. Handle each moment with the same sensitivity you would a spring flower that will wilt in the first blush of heat.

Someone once said that if we only had a sunset once a century, the whole world would turn out to see it. Tourists would travel for miles to catch it at the highest point. They would carry five kinds of cameras and telephoto lenses. It would be judged by journalists as spectacular. Special news broadcasts would interrupt the regular programming. People would talk about it for months, and nobody would miss the event. But we have sunsets every night. So while the sky grows crimson as retreating light shoots across it, we all walk blindly past. No time for sunsets. They are an endless feature of life.

Can you be wiser? Even though the present seems always upon you, it is hiding a series of last times. In a world where death is a reality, age is inevitable, and children grow up, can you clutch each moment, breathe deeply, and love tenderly? That we may have the insight to do so is my prayer for us all.

25

Over the Rainbow

During my teenage years, one of the great movie classics of all time was introduced to the public. People crowded into theaters throughout the land to see Judy Garland and an all-star cast in the *Wizard of Oz.* In the film, Judy introduced a song, "Somewhere Over the Rainbow," which remains popular to this day.

In the lyrics, the singer asks, "Over the rainbow, bluebirds fly—why, oh why, can't I?" The fact is that we really can. The time will come in the lives of all of us when we will experience death. No one is exempt. When death occurs, there will be a separation of the body and the spirit. The spirit will return to a heavenly dwelling place to await further experience and the resurrection. Perhaps that heavenly place is "over the rainbow," but the exact location does not matter. What we take with us and how we appear do matter.

With that thought in mind, don't ever underestimate the way you look. I have a friend with a great job. Because of his particular vocation, he dresses almost exclusively in conservative suits and ties and the inevitable white shirt. This man has a small son who has an equally small friend. One day as these two young tots watched the father returning home from work in his suit and tie, the little friend observed to a third small party standing by, "Why is Jason's dad always dressed for the resurrection?"

Isn't that wonderful? Somehow that little fellow has already learned that there is something beyond this life. It's a knowledge that everyone would like to have, for life could seem desolate and pointless if all the struggle and growth of this world were to end in nothing. There's a deep hunger in each of us, admitted or not, to live on. Something inside us seems eternal, indestructible. We can't help but wonder what happens to us when our bodies have worn out and stopped.

A writer interviewed hundreds of patients who had been pronounced clinically dead and then had "come back to life." He compiled what they told him about the afterlife into a book, *Life After Life,* that became an instant bestseller. You see, people want to know that life comes to more than darkness and oblivion.

May I testify to you that there is, in reality, life after death. A story by Paul Villiard that appeared in the June 1966 *Reader's Digest* illustrates what I mean. Let me share it in the author's own words.

"When I was quite young my family had one of the first telephones in our neighborhood. I remember well the polished oak case fastened to the wall on the lower stair landing. The shiny receiver hung on the side of the box. . . . I was too little to reach the telephone, but used to listen with fascination when my mother talked to it. Once she lifted me up to speak to my father, who was away on business. Magic!

"Then I discovered that somewhere inside the wonderful device lived an amazing person—her name was 'Information Please' and there was nothing she did not know. My mother could ask her for anybody's number; when our clock ran down, Information Please immediately supplied the correct time.

"My first personal experience with this genie-in-the-receiver came one day while my mother was visiting a neighbor. Amusing myself at the tool bench in the basement, I whacked my finger with a hammer. The pain was terrible, but there didn't seem to be much use crying because there was no one home to offer sympathy. I walked around the house sucking my throbbing finger, finally arriving at the stairway. The telephone! Quickly I ran for the footstool in the parlor and dragged it to the landing. Climbing up, I unhooked the receiver and held it to my ear. 'Information Please,' I said into the mouthpiece just above my head.

"A click or two, and a small, clear voice spoke into my ear. 'Information.'

" 'I hurt my *fingerrr*—' I wailed into the phone. The tears came readily enough, now that I had an audience.

" 'Isn't your mother home?' came the question.

" 'Nobody's home but me,' I blubbered.

" 'Are you bleeding?'

" 'No,' I replied. 'I hit my finger with the hammer and it hurts.'

" 'Can you open your icebox?' she asked. I said I could. 'Then chip off a little piece of ice and hold it on your finger.'

"After that, I called Information Please for everything. I asked her for help with my geography and she told me where Philadelphia was. . . . She helped me with my arithmetic, and she told me that my pet chipmunk—I had caught him in the park just the day before—would eat fruits and nuts.

"And there was the time that Petey, our pet canary, died. I called Information Please and told her the sad story. She listened, then said the usual things grown-ups say to soothe a child. But I was unconsoled: why was it that birds should sing so beautifully and bring joy to whole families, only to end as a heap of feathers, feet up, on the bottom of a cage?

"She must have sensed my deep concern, for she said quietly, 'Paul, always remember that there are other worlds to sing in.'

"Somehow I felt better.

"Another day I was at the telephone. 'Information,' said the now familiar voice.

" 'How do you spell *fix*?' I asked. . . .

"A few years later, on my way west to college, my plane put down at Seattle. I had about half an hour between plane connections, and I spent fifteen minutes or so on the phone with my sister, who lived there now. . . . Then, really without thinking what I was doing, I dialed my hometown operator and said, 'Information Please.'

"Miraculously, I heard again the small, clear voice I knew so well: 'Information.'

"I hadn't planned this, but I heard myself saying, 'Could you tell me, please, how to spell *fix*?'

"There was a long pause. Then came the softly spoken answer, 'I guess,' said Information Please, 'that your finger must have healed by now.'

"I laughed. 'So it's really still you,' I said. 'I wonder if you have any idea how much you meant to me during all that time.'

" 'I wonder,' she replied, 'if you know how much you meant to *me*? I never had any children, and I used to look forward to your calls. . . .'

" . . . I told her how often I had thought of her over the years, and I asked if I could call her again when I came back to visit my sister. . . .

" 'Please do. Just ask for Sally. . . .'

"Just three months later I was back again at the Seattle airport. A different voice answered, 'Information,' and I asked for Sally.

" 'Are you a friend?'

" 'Yes,' I said. 'An old friend.'

" 'Then I'm sorry to have to tell you. Sally had only been working part-time the last few years because she was ill. She died five weeks ago.' But before I could hang up, she said, 'Wait a minute. Did you say your name was Villiard?'

" 'Yes.'

" 'Well, Sally left a message for you. She wrote it down. . . . Here it is, I'll read it—"Tell him I still say there are other worlds to sing in. He'll know what I mean." '

"I thanked her and hung up. I *did* know what Sally meant." (Paul Villiard, "Information Please," *Reader's Digest,* June 1966, pp. 62–65.)

I want you to know that I also know what Sally meant—that there is continual life, even after mortal death. Jesus said, "Let not your heart be troubled. . . . In my Father's house are many mansions: if it were not so, I would have told you. I go to prepare a place for you." (John 14:1–2.)

Now, I also know that not only is there everlasting life but also there is, for each of us, the resurrection. Remember Job? His witness is one of the greatest. After all he went through, despite his boils and loss of possessions and family, he could say, "For I know that my redeemer liveth, and that he shall stand at the latter day upon the earth: and though after my skin worms destroy this body, yet in my flesh shall I see God" (Job 19:25–26).

Every one of us will be resurrected. It's a gift that does not discriminate. Just as spring comes to all the trees in the orchard, so will resurrection come to us. But Christ did say that there were many mansions in his kingdom. And when we are brought forth from the grave, every one of us reunited with our bodies, we will still have to be responsible for our actions on earth and be given our inheritance accordingly. Recall with me the words of the Savior: "Marvel not at this: for the hour is coming, in the which all that are in the graves shall hear his voice, and shall come forth; they that have done good, unto the resurrection of life; and they that have done evil, unto the resurrection of damnation" (John 5:28–29).

That's pretty sobering. I think if we really understand that life goes on for us after death and realize what's at stake here, we might sometimes act differently. There are other exciting worlds to sing in if we've practiced the scales.

We can each obtain a glorious resurrection. By a "glorious resurrection," I mean life again (and forever) in the presence of our Heavenly Father. I pray that the Holy Spirit will touch our hearts and witness that what I say is true. Our Eternal Father gave us this life to work out our salvation and to show him we really want to return. And we can do it. We can do it! We can repent of our sins, overcome our weaknesses, and do just a little bit better day by day until we are prepared. But there is a price, and it must be paid. It can be paid.

May we humble ourselves before our Heavenly Father and our Savior. May we seek him diligently. May our works show our commitment. May we understand that there is a resurrection and an eternal life available to us all. And above all, may we prepare ourselves so that we are truly "dressed for the resurrection."

Index